A Song for the Way

A Song for the Way

BEN HARRISON

DOMINICAN PUBLICATIONS

First published (2024) by
Dominican Publications
42 Parnell Square
Dublin 1

ISBN 978-1-905604-50-0

British Library Cataloguing in Publications Data.
A catalogue record for this book is available
from the British Library

Copyright © (2024) Ben Harrison and Dominican Publications
All rights reserved.

No part of this publication may be reproduced, stored in
a retrieval system or transmitted by any means,
electronic or mechanical, including photocopying,
without permission in writing from the publisher.

Origination and cover by Dominican Publications

Printed in Ireland by
Sprint Books, Dublin 24

Contents

Prelude
Silence or a Song   7

1. Journey   17
2. Venturing Outdoors   23
3. The Trouble with Friends   29
4. A Touch in the Darkness   38
5. Seeds from Plastic Flowers   46
6. Silence   49
7. On Being Nothing   51
8. A Dangerous Gift   57
9. Gazing into Night   65
10. Man of the Road   68
11. Musings of a Wannabe Monk   70
12. Seeing Light   74
13. Companions on the Road   78
14. A Retreat with the Enemy   84
15. Fifth and Spring   86
16. Perseverance – Just for Today   89
17. Prayer out of Passion   94

18	Like a Thief in the Night	96
19	The Burden of Self	101
20	Outgrowing Self-hatred	109
21	Vocational Vector	114
22	The Side Altar	118
23	A Memory Awakened	120
24	Landscapes, Lifescapes	123
25	Letter to Mumma	125
26	Terrible Dailiness	129
27	The Last Day of the Retreat	140
28	Bulkington Reprise	142
29	Heart to Heart	146

Postlude
A Song for the Way   146

Acknowledgements   153

Prelude
Silence or a Song

Whenever, over many years, I have thought about writing a book, I have conceived it as a song – a love song for Life, a shout of joy for its Beauty, a paean of praise to the Source of It All. But I have also conceived it as a story – the story of a journey – a log of my geographical wanderings, but even more, a grateful reflection on my search for what I might call Deep Truth, the meaning, if there is any, behind the masks and moods, the feelings and phenomena of life in this strange world of contrasts and contradictions.

So, before I start the song, before we begin the journey, I had better do what some books do and provide a map, a diagram of the terrain ahead. Because we are talking about an actual geographical sequence of movements as well as a biographical sequence of experiences, the two itineraries weave in and out of each other. So as not to anticipate events that I will describe in detail later, let me only give you a brief description of the places that we will visit.

'Home' is in a small town in the Shenandoah Valley of Virginia, just west of the Blue Ridge Mountains, where we moved when I was four. That was 1948. At that time the household consisted of my parents, Ruth and Randolph, in their early forties, and my three siblings: Shirley, nine years older, Rany Junior 11 years older, and Ruth 13 years older. My mother's mother lived with us then, and my father's mother visited occasionally. Both grandmothers died when I was about 6. I was educated in the local schools and raised in the Episcopal Church, in which my family were committed members. My mother developed cancer, and after two or three years of various treatments, died in 1956 when I was 11. This called into question everything I had been taught to believe up to that point.

Waynesboro was a small town in a beautiful location, within walking distance of fields and forests. I went to local elementary and high schools, attended a summer camp most years for kids interested in the outdoors, and went on travels with my father on his business trips. As I grew older my siblings matured and went off to college and marriage. Shirley came back to be at home after my mother died, and Lillian, dear woman, who had been hired to cook and clean when my mother got ill, continued to work for the family until after I left for college.

In those years of adolescence, I had a few friends, but spent a lot of my spare time reading the college books of my older siblings – literature, philosophy, psychology, religion – trying to make sense of life. I also spent hours in violent or heroic fantasies and, whenever the weather was half-decent, out in the forests and fields near home. Nature was a great comfort for me, although I was often lonely and confused.

My father remarried when I was about 14, and my step-mother had one daughter, the age of my older sister, and one grand-daughter the age of my oldest niece. The three of us, my father, my step-mother, whose name was Frances, and I, had a difficult time together during my remaining years at home.

At age 18, I went to the University of Maryland in College Park, in the greater Washington, D.C. area, studying literature and ancient history. I was searching for deeper meanings to life, but also avoiding being drafted for the Viet Nam war. I needed two years of therapy because of my alcoholic excesses, worked full time in a pharmacy to pay for the therapy, and was active in a Church group with a magnetic chaplain, Fr Stevens, who became a second father to me. When he died in a boating accident, what faith I had recovered was shaken to its core.

Aged 22, in the year 1966, I began my obligatory two years of active duty in the U.S. Army. My Basic and Advanced Infantry Training were in New Jersey, and I dropped out of Officer School in Virginia after one month. Then I was sent as an enlisted man to South Korea for 13 months (half in Taegu and half in Seoul). I hated the regimentation of military life but had the best friends I had known until then. We drank a lot. I finished my last five months of active time in North Carolina.

Aged 24 and surprised to find myself still alive, I got a cheap flight to Europe and hitched around the continent for four months. When I came back, I tried to settle and find work in Philadelphia, but after a year of unsatisfactory efforts, I took to the road again, hitch-hiking to San Francisco and living a semi-vagabond life of travel and tripping for a couple of years, a kind of late-blooming hippie in the Flower Power era. When I got tired of not having my own place, I settled down for another year there with a job in a freight forwarding company. That way I could have a conventional life for five days a week, and be a part-time hippie on weekends.

Then, bored and dissatisfied, aged 27, in the year 1972, I took to the road again, but, as described below, had the rock-bottom moment that drastically changed the way I approached life. Soon after, I met the director of a home for kids near Las Vegas and went for a visit. I loved it, stayed a month, and then continued my journey south into central Mexico before realizing that I was just going through the motions.

I returned and worked as a volunteer with those tough kids for five years, running errands, doing yard work, pool maintenance, driving, cooking – took the kids camping, fishing, hiking, cliff-diving in Lake Mead and Lake Mojave. As a volunteer, in addition to the enjoyable work with the kids, I had as much time as I needed out in the desert or in the mountains, reading and reflecting. I began to think about some kind of monastic or religious life and visited a number of orders in the Western U.S. In 1975 I was accepted into the Roman Catholic Church, drawn by the rich monastic and contemplative spiritual tradition of the centuries.

Finally, in July 1977, age 32, I decided to see if I had a vocation with the Missionaries of Charity Brothers, Mother Teresa's order, in Los Angeles. I didn't know if I would last a week but, here I am, 45 years later. We lived on Skid Row and worked with 'junkies, winos, ex-cons, immigrants and vagrants' – among whom I felt right at home. I was eventually appointed to train newly arriving brothers. I met Mother Teresa for the first time in 1984, just after making my final profession. I met her at least eight other times over subsequent years. After eight years in Los Angeles, I asked to try something abroad and was sent to open a house in Sicily.

We lived in Noto, a small, beautiful Baroque town near Siracusa, in Sicily, and worked with a community of local Gypsies, elderly, people with psychiatric problems, and others. I loved the work and the people there, but I also loved being out in the wild countryside and rugged hills, fragrant with wild thyme, anise and orange blossoms. I became friendly with a community of recovering addicts and realized that my addictive tendencies were still alive.

After 15 years in sun-belt countries, it was quite a shock to be sent to Manchester, England, to be the novice director for new brothers entering our order in Europe. But after six months, I found that I was also able to do something I had long wanted to do, and became a volunteer prison chaplain in Manchester Prison. I felt at home with prisoners from the first day. Providentially, I also realized that I needed some support with my addictive tendencies and started attending 12-step meetings. In addition to the help this was for me, it was providential for two other reasons: knowing about recovery gave me something practical to offer the men I was meeting 'inside', and it also showed me that there was at least one tried and proven 'way out' of the traps of addiction and criminality. I also loved my teaching work as a brother, but found that the other responsibilities entrusted to me in those years were quite burdensome.

After 16 years in Manchester, it was considered time for a change, and I was sent back to Los Angeles, where I was assigned for the next seven years, working with homeless young people in a day-centre we ran and also doing one day a week in the County Jail. My recovery contacts continued and deepened. I also began to write up some of my memories and experiences and submit them for publication.

One of the places dearest to me was the Priory, later Abbey, of Saint Andrew's in Valyermo, in the high desert north of the San Gabriel Mountains. I had visited and made retreats there for many years, since my time in Las Vegas. The monks were among the first to publish what I was writing, including some of the reflections in this book.

After those seven years in Los Angeles, during which I felt like a transplanted organ that had failed to 'take', I asked to go back to Manchester for a year, while I still knew people there, and was still relatively healthy. I was allowed to return to Manchester in 2012, and have been here ever since, making this my twelfth year back. I continue to find tremendous joy and fulfilment in my work with prisoners and in my contacts with people in addiction and recovery.

This summary of my geographical and vocational itinerary will give you something of a grid on which to locate the experiences that I chronicle in the coming pages. This is the bare skeleton. The muscle and meat of the matter are what you will find, I hope, in the pages that follow – and not only the muscle and the meat, but also the spirit and the breath that animates the ongoing journey, and the gratitude that fills my soul when I think of the people and places that I have known over these eight decades. It is because of all the blessings of these people and places, even the blessings that have been wrung out of grief and turmoil, that I want to sing this song, this song for the way. It is a song to sing along the road, but also a song to sing for the one who calls himself the Way, who is, as I say more than once in the pages that follow, my path, my companion and my destination. Amen.

≈≈

Back in the early years of Christian monasticism, there was a desert monk, Brother Zachary, who was known for humility and silence. When he was near death, the abbot Moses asked him, 'What do you see?' Zachary answered, 'Nothing better, Father, than to keep one's peace.'

Zachary's silence said a lot. To my mind, Zachary was saying that his secret relationship with God was sufficient for him. He did not want to speak of it to others, because it was none of their business, and, anyway, what can one say about such things? Perhaps also he was more aware of his unworthiness than of his exceptional gifts. In any case, Moses understood and responded, 'You are right, my son. Keep your peace.'

I have always admired people like Zachary, the hidden, quiet souls who find their identity in their relationship with God rather than by stockpiling a composite self-image from the reflected fragments of other people's impressions. There is something rock-solid yet unassuming about such people. I remember how reassured I felt when I read that Thomas Merton had selected, as a quotation for his ordination card, the passage from Genesis that speaks of Enoch: 'he walked with God.

Then he vanished because God took him.' (Genesis 5:24) That idea of vanishing had always appealed to me, and it pleased me to know that Merton had a similar fascination with it.

In my case, I would have to admit there is probably a neurotic desire to remain unnoticed or a fear of being the centre of attention. For a child, invisibility is sometimes preferable to constant criticism, and for an adult, it is preferable to constant demands. I think there is a healthy sort of hiddenness, an appropriate moment for camouflage. In basic military training, we learned very quickly to vanish into the background when the sergeant was scanning the squad for 'volunteers' to clean weapons or other menial chores. And it is sometimes a relief not to have to compete for attention or approval, to relax into an easy anonymity.

Once when we were about 13 or 14, four of us went on a camping trip. I was exploring the area while the others were setting up camp, and when I wandered back they were busy gathering wood. I climbed into Henry's hammock and lay there quietly, even when they called me. They got irritated and went off looking for me. Coming back 10 minutes later, they had begun to worry. When I coughed from the hammock, their worry turned to anger. I had enjoyed that sense of being invisible. I suppose there was an element of power, but even more than that, it was a liberating exercise for me to realize that a time will come when I am not there, when people will look for me and not find me.

I take a similar pleasure in being lost in a crowd without the need to distinguish myself, even in my own mind, from the human mass. Once I had made an appointment with a nun who ran a centre for homeless people in London, and when I got to the centre there was a long queue of men waiting to go in. I didn't want to push my way to the front and demand special treatment, so I waited peacefully in the line for nearly an hour until it was my turn to enter. I felt totally accepted and at home as one wanderer among many. And when we brothers worked in Manchester Prison, occasionally a new officer would mistake us for a couple of convicts and tell us to go to our cells – both we and our prisoner friends were delighted with this moment of undercover solidarity. Does the charm of such moments depend on the knowledge that one is not really a homeless man or a criminal? Or is it the recognition that one could very easily be either or both? Or is it the truth that in our basic humanity we are equally indistinguishable and equally original?

St Paul says that we should in some ways see ourselves as already dead with our lives 'hidden with Christ in God.' (Colossians 3:3) The hidden life has been cultivated in the history of the Church by hermits and cloistered contemplative monks and nuns, as well as by ordinary people living unobtrusively in faithfulness to their obligations. To see oneself as unexceptional is to shed the protective husk of individuality and let the naked seed fall into rich humus.

The point of all this is that there is a part of me that positively yearns for such hiddenness, anonymity and invisibility. There is part of me that wants nothing more than to be so invested in my relationship with God that I am utterly unconcerned with how others see me; and so committed to simple service to others that I am unaware of the impression I make on them. I suppose what I'm saying is that self-consciousness seems to me one of the greatest burdens of our divided human consciousness, and self-forgetfulness one of the greatest liberations.

~~~

But there is another side to my personality that wants to sing my song, that longs to tell my tale. Even at the age of 12 I was thinking of writing my adventures. I already saw life as an itinerary and wanted to chart my meanderings. At that point I suppose I fancied myself interesting enough to warrant a wide readership. Since I liked to read, as I went through the trials and sorrows of adolescence, it helped me to put things in perspective if I imagined myself as a character in a novel and thought how, as an author, I would describe my circumstances and my feelings.

As time passed, I realized that one of the things I found most interesting in the writings of others was their description of ideas and insights that I had believed up to that point to be uniquely and privately my own. It was a tremendous relief to know that others were as strange and wonderful as I. It was clear, then, that what would be of interest to others was the candid and minimally censored sharing of personal experience (even if part of a fictional narrative), not with the view of impressing others with my utter uniqueness, but with the view of making it possible for them, as well as for me, to recognize with greater clarity something previously inchoate or devalued in our awareness.

Even more than that desire to communicate there is a desire to make sense of my experience. Telling your story allows you to put incidents and insights in order, to see patterns and draw conclusions. It allows you to pre-empt the interpretation of your life, in a sense, to have first crack at deciphering the message of your journey. I have always been a meaning-monger – desperate to find purpose and direction in what happens in my life. For instance, whenever I have some sickness or physical complaint, I try to understand what God, my body or my unconscious is trying to tell me. It doesn't seem that I am willing to accept that things just happen by chance.

I am also convinced that all of the tentative and partial meanings I may find are insufficient and unconvincing. The little meanings that a person accrues through human relationships and social conventions (family bonds, friendships, accomplishments at work, creativity, knowledge, achievements), though valuable, are ultimately unsatisfactory and inadequate. The statistics regarding depression, addiction, and suicide among successful people are sufficient testimony to that. I need more than such relative, *ad hoc* meanings. I crave a final meaning, a gold-standard valuation. My life has ultimate meaning only insofar as it relates to the Ultimate itself, to God. My relationship with God *is* the meaning of my life.

So, then, the purpose of telling my story is to pour it out as a libation. The purpose of singing my song is to raise my voice in praise. But doing it, strangely, increases the effect: mysteriously, the expression of faith deepens faith and the gesture of love strengthens love. We follow the pattern set by God himself, whose tenderness abounds and overflows in Jesus, the Song of God; and then flows forth forever as a spring of living silence, a sigh of love.

Thinking about my compulsion to write, I recently asked myself what, now that I am getting old, I would like to say 'before I depart and be no more' (Psalm 39:13). And the answer came almost immediately: I want to tell other hungry, searching, dissatisfied souls that 'you can get there from here.'

What does that mean? First, 'from here' means from the particular coordinates where one is stranded, including the particular personality in which one is clothed at this point. From this exact position – being this precise person, with this predicated past and these specific qualities – you can get 'there'. When I said 'there', I didn't mean 'heaven' or 'the hereafter' or some distant, future state of bliss – I can't assure myself, much less anybody else, of reaching that destination. What I meant was that we can get to a place a few steps short of that: the threshold of the temple, the caravansary by the holy well. From there it is only a short distance to the place of seeing, the cleft in the rock – where we stand before the presence of That which cannot be described, hear the Name of the One who is Truth itself, are invited to cross the last border.

How can I say that 'you can get there from here'? Where do I get the audacity to tell you that? Because 'there' is here now! Whenever I am repentant, humble, and thankful, God is near. Any moment when I am able to let my ego identity fall aside, allow my categorical thinking to sink into the cloud of forgetting, I stand on that ledge, ready to be lifted into light.

Once I was walking in a deep valley below summer-seared cliffs in Sicily. There was a little stream burbling among the roots of towering Lombardy poplars. Far back in a tangled, shadowed bower a nightingale sang its rich, fluid song, solitary, insistent, ringing loudly up the canyon. A small, brown thrush, secretive, rarely seen, yet its song, so poignant, so powerful, split the noonday heat asunder like a ripped veil. It said to me, 'You can get there from here, from here, from this very here.' And the silence responded, like whispering water, 'Here. This very here.' The silence and the song continued their antiphonal exultation. And my soul, in silence, shouted, 'Here!'

1
Journey

One of the first entire books I read as a child of eight was about a lost boy wandering the countryside in search of home. One of the first stories I wrote as a boy of nine was about a cat that ambled aboard a ship and made a circuit of the world. Already at age 10 I was listing the states I passed through with my father going on his business trips and to his summer conventions. When people asked me what I wanted to do when I grew up, the only consistent answer I was able to come up with was 'a photographer for *National Geographic*.' Being on the road has always captured my imagination, and one of my favourite images for life is the journey, the pilgrimage.

For three years after I finished college and did my obligatory stint in the Army, travelling was my primary occupation. Since I didn't have much money, I did as many young people did back then and hitchhiked the roads of Europe and America. You put out your hand or your thumb, indicating you needed a lift. Sometimes you held up a sign showing your destination. Most cars would drive right by, especially those with families and middle-aged women. But fairly often someone would stop, another young person, a business man on a long drive, a construction worker, a truck driver. This mode of travel was, for me, an experiment in learning how my plans and desires might mesh with those of other people. Though I was not religious *per se*, this way of travelling was also a testing of Providence and of the notion of living in the present moment, taking 'no thought for the morrow'.

There are few feelings as liberating for a young man in good health as venturing out to the highway on a bright, sunny morning, not knowing what adventures await him. The only thing you have to do before the day is over is find something to eat and somewhere to roll out your sleeping bag, even if only under a bridge or in the back of somebody's car. You live in the present. You pore over your maps, dream of distant byways, compare notes with other travellers, but you pretty much live in the day. Perhaps that's why it's called 'journey' – the distance you can travel in *un jour*.

But I have to admit, by the end of the day, whether I'd had good luck and covered hundreds of miles or plodded the whole day with only a few short hops, I was looking with a certain amount of envy at those going home from work to houses with lights on and evidence of activity in the kitchen. The exhilaration of setting out in the mornings was matched by a certain loneliness and nostalgia as the dark descended. One of the starkest lessons learned on my travels is that I am capable of being miserable anywhere, even in the most idyllic settings.

From the autumn of 1968 (when, at age 24, I finished my two years of active duty in the Army) till the spring of 1972, I covered thousands of miles this way. My first long trip during this period was a four-month tour of Europe, which I began by hitching to Philadelphia and New York, then flying to Luxemburg and doing a leisurely circuit of Britain and Ireland. Then I hitched with a young woman friend from the French port of Dieppe on the Channel, north to Amsterdam, down the Rhine, across to Salzburg and Vienna, down the Dalmatian coast and over the mountains to Skopje and on to Athens. From there my friend, ill after the long slog, flew home to Britain, and I continued for a couple of weeks exploring a few of the islands and the Peloponnesus. Then I was off across snowy mountain roads through central Greece to Corfu, by ship to the heel of Italy, and back through Rome, Florence and Paris to Dover and London. I still treasure the memories and the lessons of those four months. Perhaps the greatest realization of that trip was that I could survive risks and realize my dreams.

Then, after a year back in the eastern United States (with a few trips north and south from Philadelphia), I hitched in mid-winter from Philadelphia to Los Angeles and on to San Francisco, which was still the haven of hippies. Along the way I paid flying visits to some of my Army buddies. The summer of that same year (1970) I travelled by back roads from the San Francisco Bay Area to Glacier National Park, and then by U.S. Route 2 across Montana and the northern tier to the northern peninsula of Michigan (rife with black-flies), and then on across Ontario to Montreal, then south to Virginia.

After a few weeks with my family, my step-mother said, 'When you said you were going to "bum around", I didn't think you meant it so literally.' I hitched back to New York, did a circuit to Quebec City, out to New Brunswick, back through Maine, a side-trip to Cape Cod and on to West Park, New York. After a month seeing what life in a monastery there was like, I made my way back across the continent via Chicago, Omaha, Denver and Reno to San Francisco. That last trip, the night before my departure from New York, I had 28 cents in my pocket when a college friend (who providentially turned up at the monastery that same evening) slipped me a 10-dollar bill for the road. Thus I hitched across the continent three times in one year, in addition to numerous side-excursions up and down the California coast.

Since those days of maximum liberty, I have hitched occasionally when I needed to get somewhere and didn't have money or couldn't find public transport. I wouldn't hesitate to do it in an emergency even now, in my seventies. But the occasion I want to talk about happened in the winter of 1972, when I was 27. After the year of the three cross-country tours (1970) I had decided to get a job, and ended up working at an international freight-forwarding company in San Francisco. After a little over a year of experimenting with a more regulated lifestyle – working Monday to Friday and playing the part-time hippie on weekends – I found myself feeling trapped and dissatisfied. I had read several books about cheap adventure travel in Latin America and decided, for lack of anything I really wanted to do, that I would hitch-hike to Mexico, and then see how far I could get moving south, on local buses, trains or whatever transportation I could find. Would I, as one friend suggested, be eaten by goats in Guatemala? Die of malaria trying to get through the jungles of Darien between Panama and Colombia? Get lost amidst the villages in the Andes or the backwaters of the Amazon? Would I make it to the Pampas, the Chilean Alps, the windswept wilds of Tierra del Fuego? Would I find a wife, a career, a prison cell, a revolution? Addiction, madness, a violent end?

The first day I made it as far as Santa Cruz. There are dozens of details and stories to tell in all this, but they are for other occasions. It was the season when acacias were blooming, and the air was redolent of their dusty sweetness. I slept poorly that first night because of a bawling baby in the next room. The second day I got a lift to Monterey and another to somewhere past Carmel, where my luck failed. I can tell you the day – it was Thursday 17 February, 1972. If I were to borrow a car and drive south from Carmel, I just might be able to find the spot, certainly I could place it within a mile or two, even now, all these years later.

I had walked, trudged, for an hour, maybe two. The Coast Highway in that area is a two-lane road used mostly by tourists and a few locals, and tourists don't usually give lifts to strange, long-haired vagabonds. So it wasn't surprising, really, that no cars were stopping, even slowing down. Anyway, I was probably giving off angry 'vibes', miserable and disgruntled and taking it personally that no one would look my way. As a car would approach, I'd face it and hold out my thumb. The drivers didn't even look at me. After a while, as they drove by, I'd flip them off. After a few more rejections I got so angry I picked up a discarded beer bottle and threw it against a rock by the road. A few more cars whizzed past and the final straw! I shouted out a long string of oaths and expletives ending with the words 'Jesus Christ!'

I considered myself an atheist, certainly not a believer. But I did have a certain interest in spirituality, and, in fact, was hoping to spend the next few nights at a Catholic monastery in Big Sur that I had heard about from a hippie poet in a North Beach café. He said the monks would let you stay a few days free, if you said you had no money.

A split second after I said 'Jesus Christ!', prompted by some impish trickster in my mind, I found myself saying, with a confident smirk, 'Okay, Jesus Christ, you're supposed to be such a hot shot. You get me a ride here and I'll give my life to you – maybe!'

A few seconds later, before I had time to register what had just come out of my mouth, a small, yellow Datsun pick-up screeched to a stop beside me, two young construction workers in the cab. 'Hop in back. Where ya' goin'?'

'The monastery.'

'Right, we're passing there.'

Once I had thrown my pack in and climbed in the back of that truck, felt the wind in my hair and delighted in the open views of towering redwoods, fragrant mountains dropping off to crashing surf and the far horizon of the vast Pacific, I forgot my frustration, my anger, and my 'maybe' promise. I felt free again. But in those next three days at the monastery, in the dense silence of bees buzzing in the chaparral and the thud of the surf pounding against the cliffs a thousand feet below, I pondered long and hard about the direction of my life.

All those years of chasing happiness had left me lost, depressed, at risk of doing damage to myself through drugs, dangerous liaisons, or hazards encountered on mountain roads and urban alleys. What if it were true that happiness comes in giving, not receiving? I could see that *my* choices, *my* will, had led me to a dead end. What if I tried to be open to somebody else's will? God's will? Fate? Destiny? Chance? I didn't know. But during those days I tentatively began to ask whatever was there to show me the way and help me to be open to whatever awaited me. If I remember correctly, I actually used the words, 'Teach me to love.'

Looking back, I can see that from that moment my life changed. From that day the random wandering of a lost soul became a journey, a daily trek on a pilgrimage toward a holy place, a home, a hearth. From that day, the road became a Way and the one whose name I took in vain has become my best friend and my constant companion. I don't know if the fact that the pick-up stopped at that moment was God's answer to my cheeky challenge. It certainly wasn't convincing enough to convert me on the spot. But somehow that chink in the armour of my self-will allowed a playful spirit to slip in and slowly begin to change me, to soften me, to free me.

I do not say that I recognized his presence right away. It took months before I began to understand that it was he, and years before I understood well exactly who he was. But from those first days in Big Sur, I was open to his leading. When I left the monastery to continue my southward journey, I made a conscious intention, in effect a prayer, to 'go with the flow', to let life live me. Looking back, I see that he set the course and has kept me to it, despite my frequent rebellion, stubbornness, fear and hesitation.

In the moments of scepticism and uncertainty, I find myself saying to him, 'Looking at the whole sweep of my life, I have to admit that you've done a better job of organizing this journey than I ever managed.' When I didn't know what to do with myself and was on the point of throwing my life away, I said, in effect, 'If you're there and you can do anything with this mess, it's yours.' And he has given me a little something to do every day since then.

So now, as the long journey continues, I am happy to say each day, 'Go ahead, my Friend. Lead on!'

2
Venturing Outdoors

Even in my earliest memories I can detect a difference between my feelings about the world of people and the world of nature. I would say that even from the age of two or three, I experienced family life, my first immersion in social realities, as a place rife with tensions, demands and expectations – and the world of gardens, pastures and woodlands as places of respite. Oh, there was the incident of the charging bull, but that was an exception.

I don't believe our family was any more fraught with tensions than any household harbouring three teenagers and one young child. And I certainly don't want to suggest that I wasn't loved. On the contrary, with three siblings older than me (by nine, 11, and 13 years), I was positively doted upon. Most of the time they treated me as their little pet, though there were times when I was just a pest. I remember when I was about two, my sister Shirley took me on a walk in a shady street and hushed me to listen to the soft plaint of the mourning doves. My brother Rany took me on an expedition through a field thick with wild flowers to the barn where the bull lived.

From very early, in family, neighbourhood, school and small-town life, I found social realities, though at times reassuring, also, often, conflictive. My tendency was to take refuge in nature, maybe I could even say, to seek a relationship with the world beyond the confines of society. I suppose even then I was an introvert, a budding contemplative. I was fascinated by the little world of mossy tree roots and ants on flagstone walkways. I would play with broken bricks under the lilac boughs and watch the wren singing from his little *terra cotta* pot nest. All of my family loved the outdoors and, on our walks, pointed out curiously shaped rocks, twisted trees and striking landscapes. When interpersonal relations got stressful, my first response was to turn to the world of nature.

After the trauma of my mother's death when I was 11, first I turned in on myself and became something of a loner. But when my father remarried a couple of years later, I was more and more out, in all weathers, wandering alone or with a friend through our tree-lined streets, down along our little river, out across cornfields and cow pastures, and into the deeply forested mountains that were only a 40-minute walk from home. That feeling of being a misfit, common to so many teenagers, drove me to seek comfort in these solitary escapes. I suppose my adolescent angst was exacerbated by a deep sense that somehow my mother's death was a sign that I wasn't worthy of love. Of course, my family tried to compensate for that loss, but a mother's love is irreplaceable.

So, when my proper Protestant monotheism and the gentle Christian faith of my elementary school years had been thus violently shattered by my mother's death, I put all that childish credulity aside and began to seek other ways to make sense of reality. It seems that, even as a youth, I needed some sort of metaphysical framework into which to slot my life, to find some sense of fitting into the larger scheme of things.

As I entered my teens, the solace I found in nature became more focused. First I tried worshipping the gods of nature. I wrapped myself in my green, brown and yellow Indian blanket and bowed to the rising sun. I gazed at the moon, charted its phases and gave my mind and heart to the tidal influence of its pull. I built a little altar of stones in the back yard, with a view of the winter-grey ridge of mountains huddled like hierophants over the rolling farmland of the Shenandoah Valley. I read about medicinal and magical plants and concocted potions hoping, long before the psychedelic age, to journey outside myself or deep within. I wrote a hymn to the god of death. But all of these experiments lacked the authenticity of those other moments of emergent clarity that came unbidden as I watched the river slide, silver, by the bending reeds, or listened to the wind clacking the bare limbs of locust trees on a stormy winter night.

Even now, I can be seized by an almost heart-breaking sense of tenderness when I come across an ancient tree with its roots roped around an outcrop of rocks; or a pile of stones with a few clumps of long grass and bramble sprouting among them in the shaded corner of a field; or a low, moss-covered wall by a brick walkway in a neglected graveyard.

These moments of insight, these intuitive glimpses of a Presence, of the underlying oneness of all things, helped me survive the loneliness, loss and self-loathing that cohabited my struggling, adolescent soul. I suppose there was a natural progression from seeing the forces of nature as distinct powers toward seeing the unity lying beyond or beneath them. At one point in my mid-teens I called myself a pantheist, and the creed I formulated read, 'I am because I am and because I am part of God, who is only because he is.'

That concept of being, that abstraction from all separate things toward a principle of is-ness, was the bedrock of my natural faith. I had no patience with the conventional, personal God of my Christian up-bringing precisely because that concept was freighted with so much social and interpersonal tension, laden with so many demands, duties and prohibitions. But I hungered for some kind of deeper, unifying vision that could embrace and harmonize the conflicts within me.

Then I started reading Alan Watts on Zen and was transported into that paradoxical place beyond all dichotomies, even the one between being and nothingness. Aldous Huxley's *The Perennial Philosophy*, recommended by a Quaker friend, introduced me more deeply to the mystical view of life. My spiritual search always teetered along the border between the personal, social reality of my emotionally charged relationships with people on one hand and the more open, impersonal world of nature on the other. Even now as an old man, I straddle that divide, still feel the stress that the claims of people and society arouse in me, still find comfort in what carries me beyond that place of tension and distress – the meta-social, the metaphysical, the transcendent.

Skipping ahead a few years, in university I had studied literature and ancient history, always with an eye to the deeper truths embedded in art and culture. After seeing how the wisdom of the Egyptians and Babylonians influenced the Hebrew Scriptures and how the philosophy of classical Greece and Rome prepared the ground into which Christianity was born, I took a course on the Dead Sea Scrolls. It was a small class, taught by a rabbi, and I was the only non-Jew. It was a fascinating experience. And it was while reading for that class that the deeper meaning of Exodus 3:14 hit me for the first time.

Moses, an outcast and a wanderer far from the family tents, in the midst of barren wilderness, has a mystical experience, an encounter with the Absolute, and that mysterious One reveals himself as 'I Am', as 'He Who Is'. For the first time I realized powerfully that it was just possible that the abstract principle of being that I had settled on as my ultimate truth, what Pascal called the God of the philosophers, might also be the Holy One whom the Bible revealed. In that case, God was not the anthropomorphic projection of social norms as caricatured by conventional religion, but was the paradoxical, ineffable Absolute experienced by mystics and lovers.

These insights from my youth help me even now. These past weeks my community has been dealing with bureaucracies regarding passports, visas and permissions required for our work with prisoners and homeless people. My neurotic insecurities arouse deep anxieties – fear of failure, disapproval, rejection – not only on the part of governments and agencies but also by colleagues and confreres. Though I know that I exaggerate these fears and that they pose little real danger, I still feel the stress. What helps? A walk in the winter sunshine, early buds on forsythia bushes, a mistle thrush singing from a chimney pot, and the knowledge that our little planet continues faithfully circling its sun. My worth does not derive from how well I succeed in dealing with bureaucrats, nor even from how well I perform my duties, but in the fact that I balance my way along the ledge between being me and being naught; and that on either side of that ledge is – what is his name? – 'Who Is!'

What we call nature, all that lies beyond the walls of our social construct and sometimes pushes its tendrils through the bricks, has, then, since my earliest years, been the comforting presence to which I turned when beset and besieged by the expectations of other humans. Sometimes I found on my hikes moments of laughter at the antics of a stoat, awe at the rolling dive of a raven, or serenity resting my gaze, from a high rock, on the multi-textured leaf-patterns of the Eastern deciduous forests. There were rare, fleeting instants of ecstasy, when I was overpowered by the desire to unite myself passionately, body and soul, with the sensuous contours of rolling mountains, or immerse myself in a pool beneath a desert waterfall, or swim in the fish-filled swells of a tropical sea. But often my solitary searches to recapture that peace were wrung with the anguish of loneliness or frantic longing for a friend. I could accept creation as it was, why could I not accept myself? Why was I so lonely? Why did I feel so unlovable? How could the judgments and condemnations of elders and peers contaminate the pure bond with the elemental world that first spawned my being?

I was only three or four, and I was in the pasture across from our house on St Charles Avenue, watching my sister and her friend climbing in an apple tree. Mute with fear, I saw the black bull coming, and they did not, until it was bearing down on us. Shirley instantly dropped from the tree, grabbed me and ran for the fence. We both rolled under just as he came to a thundering halt at the barbed wire barrier. Shirley's friend was marooned in the tree until the bull got bored and strolled back to his barn. It really happened. It wasn't a dream. I asked, and Shirley remembers it clearly.

Nature is spoken of as a mother, and she often nurtures and caresses her children. But sometimes, absent-mindedly, she bites off heads and gnaws on limbs. I love her, but I watch her moods. A few years ago, walking along the cliffs at St Bee's Head, I saw the limp, black necks of 11 guillemots crushed under a rock shelf that had collapsed on the ledge on which they were nesting. Below, the surf churned and sucked against the rocks as always.

As a young man I craved union with the cosmos, and I writhed with longing to be free of the burden of myself. I was a child of nature and yet felt trapped in it. Sometimes it seemed like a welcoming friend, but other times it looked at me through eyes glazed with indifference, or even with overt hostility. Trekking in the Lake District a few years ago, I realized that I find scenes of unadulterated nature, containing no human artefact, forbidding and scary. There needs to be some small sign of human presence, as in an oriental landscape – a bit of a stone wall, a path over a plank bridge, an abandoned shed.

It may seem that I have confused two notions. The idea that I sought comfort in nature may seem to be intertwined with the idea that I sought solace in what transcends nature. But as I reflect more deeply,

I see that these are two stages of the same movement, the movement outwards – first out of the doors of home and town into nature, then out of the doors of the created world to whatever lies beyond.

What lies beyond that door? Scientists propose that there was nothing before the big bang. Is that void, that Nada, the context in which our universe is still expanding? Do we use a capital N for that nothing? When I go out of doors from my status as a creature, do I find some nirvanine peace? Is there an icy emptiness or a welcoming warmth? Is the nothing that stands beyond creation a principle, a mystery, a banality? Can I speak of it? To it? I to Thou? Or is silence my only option? Or a scream of terror? Or a groan of woe? Or a sigh of surrender? Am I trapped?

Perhaps both of these manners of going out parallel a more basic movement – the going out from myself, the escape from the tangles of my fear-driven self-absorption. For I can imagine no fate worse than dying trapped forever in myself. To have no hope of release from that prison would be hell indeed. Maybe that is the intuition that lies at the core of all human fear of death – the recognition that nothing is more frightening than being inescapably walled in by one's own loneliness and self-recrimination.

And nothing fills me with a sense of exultation more than the thought that someday I may be liberated from the narrow confines of my own self-consciousness – that I may be given some sense of the height and depth and breadth of the spiritual freedom that is the gift promised to a heart longing to go out from itself in love. When I open the door of self, I find a path, a way that winds through valleys of shadows and light, in the company of a friend, to that other door, the gate that leads to the freedom where conflicts cease, where peace is restored, where we are home at last with all that is, and with the One Whose going out from self is the deepest source of all that is.

3

The Trouble with Friends

Standing by the corner of our privet hedge I shouted, 'Jody!' But then I remembered he was gone. His family had moved away. We had been friends for a few months in the summer when we were five, and then I never saw him again.

Jimmy, the boy across the street, seemed a bit strange to me, but we played together a lot. One day his grandmother yelled at us for making too much noise and we chased her with shovels. I guess we were going to clobber her, but Jimmy's mother intervened, and when she informed my mother, I was reprimanded severely.

When I was about seven, I brought Gavin home from school one afternoon. My parents were out. Gavin and I got a big, iron model car that had been passed down to me and smashed big dents in it with rocks. Then we decided it would be a good idea to break all twelve panes out of the window in the side of the garage. There was no malice in this act of vandalism, but when my father's face appeared in the broken glass, I somehow realized that it hadn't been a good idea. Gavin was suddenly nowhere to be seen, and I was left to suffer the consequences alone. It seems that Gavin was not considered a good influence and was henceforth unwelcome at our house.

On another occasion, playing with Jimmy in my sand box, I was curious to know what would happen if I let a big iron fence post fall against his head. I thought it out during lunch and, that afternoon, got him to lean over to move a brick in the sand, and then I let the post fall in his direction. My calculations were exact. When the pole made contact, Jimmy started screaming, and I tried to shush him, saying, 'Don't be a cry-baby!' But then I saw the red tide come surging through his short-cropped hair, and his mother came running and rushed him off for stitches.

There were plenty of occasions on which I played nicely with other children, both in school and in the neighbourhood, but for some reason I remember these shameful occasions. Perhaps that is because they were the moments when I learned unforgettable lessons. I don't remember which of my friends joined me in the great turtle hunt. We found a box turtle in the back yard and decided we should impale it with a large iron spear that was used for breaking ice. We were standing over the poor little creature as though we had slaughtered a dragon when my sister came out to see what we were up to and expressed her disgust at our wanton brutality.

I have been criticized for using the word 'friend' too loosely, and also for not having enough friends my own age and social group. Perhaps growing up with older siblings and having their comrades around made it easy for me to relate to people older than I. In high school, during the summers I worked with younger children at a nature-study camp and got along well with them too. Besides feeling at ease with kids older and younger than myself, I was not generally over-awed by people in authority, and enjoyed telling slightly off-colour jokes to my teachers. The people I could not bring myself to make friends with were those of my own age who were the confident go-getters. They scared me because they were more aggressive and more physically adept than I. And these were precisely the kids my parents thought I should count as my friends, the children of their equals and associates. Instead, I seemed to gravitate toward the kids who were from the wrong side of the tracks, those from unstable families, or those who were the more studious types we called 'egg-heads.'

My uncle and aunt continued to visit occasionally after my mother died. My uncle obviously remembered the crazy days when my older brother and sisters lived at home and always had a posse of their friends studying together, partying, playing music and dancing. But those days were long passed, and it was only me at home now, age 13, with my father, when he wasn't on a business trip, and the younger of my sisters, who was at college all day and studying at night. When this uncle and auntie visited, the house must have seemed unusually quiet. He asked, 'Where are your friends?' Caught by surprise, I mumbled something about their not coming to our house much. He continued,

'Your father says you don't have any.'

That was a punch in the gut. Didn't I? I think I did. It's true, I was what I later discovered was called an introvert, and had always needed a lot of time to process what was happening in my life. No doubt, my mother's death still weighed on me and contributed to the sombre mood of our house. But I did have good friends, usually one or two, of both sexes. Sometimes after a year or two they moved away or we grew apart, but there were always a few of my peers with whom I could talk, in whom I could confide, who shared my interest in nature, in books, in trying to make sense of life.

At university, after a bashful beginning I really enjoyed dormitory life and also the companionship in the Church group I was part of. I suppose that's when I really learned the importance of friendships and some of the skills needed to live alongside roommates and neighbors I would never have chosen on my own. And my time in the army showed me how shared adversity cemented bonds of affection. My army buddies were certainly the closest friends I had known up to that point. In the years when I was travelling around and working at odd jobs, friendships were more provisional. But it sometimes happens that, with people you meet 'on the road' and with whom you share the bread of the journey, you discover an almost instantaneous trust that allows you to confide hopes and fears that are too personal to divulge even to life-long acquaintances.

In my late twenties, I went through a period when I felt very lonely. There were many people around me whom I cared for and who I knew cared about me, but there was a longing for deeper intimacy. I needed someone to whom I could reveal not just my deepest secrets, but even my most cherished hopes: someone in whose presence I could let the tide of my willing subside completely, leaving an empty beach.

Sometimes it felt that, since my mother's death, there was nobody I could rely on to desire my mere existence. It had been my mother's desire for another child that led to my conception, and it was her love that had kept me alive through all my childhood illnesses and perils. After she died, I felt that it was I myself alone whom I had to rely on to keep willing my existence. Was there no one, no friend, no other human being, who would take on the burden of holding me in existence by their simple but steadfast desire for my mere presence in this world?

At one point, the loneliness grew so intense that I wrote my brother to see if he could explain it. I wondered if there might be something about my early childhood that would account for my sense of alienation. Was I illegitimate? Was I unwanted, an accident? Was I adopted? Had some unremembered trauma scarred me? My older brother was always out-going, friendly, active, engaged with people. He was popular, fun-loving, by this time a responsible married man with a wife and children, a respected university professor, a person with an array of social contacts, hobbies and interests. In so many ways I had always felt overshadowed and inadequate following in his path. Teachers, shop-keepers, people at Church called me by his name. But my uncle, all those years before, had been able to see the difference – I was the one with no friends.

When the answer to my letter came, it said, 'My dear brother, there is nothing wrong with you, there was nothing odd about your birth. You were wanted from the beginning. We human beings are all lonely at times, and for many of us, if we are honest, there is a loneliness at the very heart of us.'

His words reassured me, though it took many years of further painful pining before I learned to accept my loneliness as 'just part of life'. The deeper that acceptance has become, the better a friend I have been to others. Perhaps even more importantly, that acceptance has allowed me to turn to God. It seems to me that the human heart has a need for an unlimited amount of love, and there is only one unlimited supply. The loneliness I still often feel is a pledge of the bond I have with my Lord. As hunger can be pleasurable when it comes as a result of strenuous efforts and when there is plenty of food in the larder, so also that ordinary loneliness can remind us of the joy that will soon come when we can bask again in the presence of the One who loves us without limit. And when I say soon, I am not thinking of some distant, heavenly bliss but of the sense of well-being that visits us occasionally when we open our hearts to his grace.

When I told a recovery friend, over coffee, that I was thinking of writing on friendship, I confessed to her that I was a bit daunted at the prospect. I don't feel that I have any expertise on the subject. In fact, someone who was close to me once told me that I am too selfish to be a real friend to anybody. In retrospect, I think that was a cruel bit of manipulation, but it sowed a seed of doubt that niggles still.

As I talked with my friend, I was surprised at how much we shared on the level of fear. We both hesitate to call people friends or to profess ourselves friends even of people we are close to. There is a fear that we will not be able to live up to their expectations, or they to ours; a fear of rejection, a fear of not being loved equally, a fear of disappointing or being disappointed. In our highly fluid society and our emotionally beleaguered psychological ambient, you wonder how long anybody is going to remain accessible and interested.

The ability to share these things with my friend in recovery reminds me of an observation I hear often in recovery meetings, that for many of us the skills we learn in our programme are what allow us to have true, deep friendships for the first time. As I experience the healing assurance that I struggle with the very same fears and failings as others, I learn to accept myself, to lower my defences and to reveal my inner thoughts and feelings, through the transparency and vulnerability the twelve-step programme expects of me.

There is also the question of levels of friendship. Who are merely associates, colleagues or acquaintances; who are companions, comrades, buddies; and who are real friends? Who are those rare few of whom the Bible says we are fortunate to have one or two such friends in a lifetime. Who is the Jonathan to my David, the one for whom I would give my life?

When I first joined the brothers, about age 33, in the early months of my novitiate, our novice director said something that made a big impact on me. He said, 'If you want to be friends with someone, you have to waste a lot of time with them. So if you want to be friends with Jesus, you have to waste a lot of time in the chapel.' In fact, I think it probably often works the other way as well. You find somebody with whom you are inclined to waste time and eventually, when you've shared enough experiences of various kinds, you discover that you have become friends. For me, the irony of using the words 'waste time' was perfect, because I am often tempted to lose myself in purposes and projects. It is sometimes hard for me just to spend time with somebody for the pleasure of it.

Since childhood, especially when I went to New York or other big cities with my father on his business trips, I had been drawn to churches open on weekdays when there was no service on. I liked the quiet, the dark, and the sense of presence. It felt as though someone was there, someone whose language was silence, whose longing was to listen. The flickering of candles in the darkness mirrored the warmth and movement of life. If a few people were about, engaged quietly in their devotions, lighting candles or praying the Stations of the Cross, busy at their own private dealings with God, it helped me realize that each soul had a private claim on Whoever dwelt in that quiet place, each had a unique bond with Whatever waited in the innermost recesses of that stillness.

In his reflections in *The Four Loves*, C.S. Lewis says that one of the characteristics of the love that is called friendship is that friends often stand beside each other, looking at something that interests them both. Since my first rock-bottom experience at the age of 27, referred to in the chapter titled 'Journey' above, the daily companion of my journey has been Jesus. A companion is one with whom you share your bread, and Jesus has been the one who shared my daily ration of meaning and mystery. It is not surprising that someone with whom you share sustenance over a long period, and whom you come to know intimately, becomes a friend. That sense of his being beside me is not always intense, but, in a way, you can take a good friend for granted. You can shift your interest to the work at hand, or to the view ahead, or to the song of the blackbird you both enjoy.

There have been many occasions when I was very much aware of Jesus standing by me – occasions when he defended me in danger, or supplied the courage I needed to face a challenge, or comforted me when I felt I could go no further. And there are the occasions when two friends need to face each other and look deep into each other's eyes – to see if there is understanding, trust, hurt, uncertainty.

How do you get to know someone in this way, who is not visibly present to you, into whose eyes you can only gaze metaphorically? How do I know that he is not merely my 'imaginary friend', some psychological figment compensating for my affective deprivation?

I would say you get to know Jesus by reading about him, first of all in the Scriptures, and then what is written or said about him by his friends, the greatest of whom are those called saints, who have come to share not only his mind and his heart, but also his closeness to his Father. And I know him through the Church and its sacraments and teaching. How better to get to know him than to live, each year, through the liturgy, the entire trajectory of his life among us, which had only one purpose, to communicate to us that he wants us to be his friends? But beyond all that, ruminating on all that, it is in wasting time with him in the cell of my heart that I experience his daily nearness, not often in swoony feelings but in the down-to-earth, ordinary awareness of faith. It is all this that convinces me that my experience of Jesus is real, and the fact that millions of Christians through hundreds of years have had a remarkably consistent experience of this man Jesus, who embodies and reveals all the goodness of God.

Whenever I think at any depth about friendship, I remember a sermon I heard in a Baptist church in Washington D.C., back in the days of the civil rights movement. The preacher was talking about two elderly women whom he had known for many years. When one of them died he was surprised that the other didn't seem much bothered by the loss. So he said to her, 'Annie May, I thought you and Martha were the best of friends! You were always sitting on the front porch laughing and joking together. But you don't seem much upset by her passing. Why is that?'

'Well, Reverend,' she responded, 'she was a fine woman, but I wouldn't call her my best friend. You can laugh with anybody. A friend is the one you can cry with.'

Walking day by day these many years in the company of Jesus, since that desperate day when I first shouted his name, he has become my best friend, my friend of friends, who laughs with us and cries with us. I have wasted many hours with him. I have come to know him through my incorporation in his very body, the Church, but also through the radical acceptance and love he has shown me through others. I have learned that, confident of his acceptance, I can open my heart to my fellow pilgrims; can admit my hopes and fears to them knowing that our shared humanity neutralizes the shame of weakness. Recognizing him hidden in my fellow travellers, I have had the joy of serving him and being close to him in those I work with. Some of those have honored me by calling me their friend, and by that honour have given me the courage to call them friends in return. There is that classic definition of the Christian as one beggar telling another where to find bread. Or, maybe we could say, one lonely soul telling another where their friend is waiting.

When speaking to that same recovery friend I mentioned before, I told her how deeply it touches me that my prisoners and addicts and friends in recovery trust me with precious confidences. I don't feel worthy of it, and I was wondering what it was about me that inspired their trust. Good friend that she is, she didn't hesitate to challenge my presumption: 'Maybe it's nothing to do with you. Maybe it's who is *with* you.' That put me in my place – exactly where I want to be.

Not long ago, when I was struggling yet again with that sense of loneliness that we so often interpret as worthlessness, I had this thought: if my best friend was willing to die for me, how can I doubt that I am loved, or lovable. One of my favourite Holy Week hymns says it well:

> He came from his blest throne,
>   Salvation to bestow;
> But men made strange, and none
>   The longed-for Christ would know;
>   But oh, my Friend,
>   My Friend indeed,
>   who at my need
>   His life did spend!

And a few verses later the hymn continues:

> Here might I stay and sing,
>   No story so divine;

Never was love, dear King,
  Never was grief like Thine.
    This is my Friend
    In whose sweet praise
    I all my days
    Would gladly spend.

                Samuel Crossman (1623-83)

4

A Touch in the Darkness

It was more than 60 years ago, but I remember it clearly. My sister woke me and took me into her room and was showing me the trinkets on her dresser when my father came in. He spoke to her over my head and asked, 'Have you told him?' She shook her head. He sat with me on the bed and said, with a sob, 'Son, God has taken Mumma home to heaven.' I had never seen him choked up before, but still I was hurt that he could say that her 'home' was so far from us.

That was the watershed moment of my life. Nothing was the same after that. The roomy, comfortable surroundings of my childhood proved themselves a cheap, painted stage-set, a canvas backdrop ripped and tattered by a falling beam. Behind it, the bare brickwork, pulleys and coiled ropes, the machinery of illusion, were exposed for all to see. I went to my room, climbed back in bed, grabbed the little terry-cloth pillow *she* had made for me and cried into it until it was sodden.

I was 11. But in that moment I felt like a grown tree, wind-struck and storm-broken. Sometimes I have been with a young family and suddenly realized that their child was 11 years old. It always surprises me to see how small, how fragile 11 looks.

It was spring and hyacinths were blooming on the day of her burial. Their scent still awakens that ancient sorrow. It was deemed best for me not to go to the funeral – I don't know, perhaps they were afraid that I would blubber. As far as I remember, nobody explained to me what had happened, how she had died, or how I was expected to react, and I went to school as usual the following Monday. I will not recount here the long story leading up to that moment except to say that the vibrant household of my pre-school days had been sobered and silenced by Mumma's long struggle with cancer, and by my older sisters' and

A reflection on bereavement and vocation

brother's gradual departure for college and eventual marriage. Rather, what I want to reflect on is how my mother's death influenced my spiritual search and my vocation.

I sometimes think that her loss is what caused me to start thinking about the great questions of good and evil, of good fortune and suffering, and to start searching for the truth that underlay the social conventions and familial illusions that seemed so false in the light of her death. We had been a church-going family, and we had prayed every evening that God would 'bless Mumma and make her well.' I had not had any doubts that he would do so. So when she died I had to conclude that either God wasn't there or he was weak, or heartless. I found no solace in the faith that had seemed so reassuring to me shortly before. I was also beginning to feel the impulses of adolescence and I didn't want to believe, as some suggested, trying to comfort me, that my mother was still watching over me. I didn't want her to see what I was getting up to. Though there were other people around and some were kind to me even at great personal sacrifice, they were all moving on their own paths, and I still felt a terrible loneliness, rejection and fear. Life seemed utterly empty.

In my early teens I liked the sombre stories of Poe and de Maupassant, drew pictures of knives and guns, dreamed of being a ruthless gangster, lost myself in violent fantasies, wrote stories where people died of snake-bites or were impaled on spikes or crushed under piles of jagged rocks. Later, I was drawn to the works of Melville and Dostoevsky and started reading books about philosophy and psychology, in search of some deeper understanding of the human condition. And I began smoking, drinking, and sniffing glue. The few friends I had must have found me a heavy presence. I was the thinker, the contemplative, the philosopher. I found some relief in solitary wanderings in the mountains and fields near home and satisfied my spiritual longings through a kind of pantheistic nature mysticism and an interest in Zen. By the time I finished high school, I had concluded that there was no God and life was a meaningless drudgery that I was too cowardly to end and too venal to discipline into stoical endurance.

Despite that, when I started college, I gravitated toward a student

Church group under the pastoral care of a magnetic chaplain. After a year of non-judgmental acceptance and friendship in that small community, I gained the trust to unburden myself to Fr S. He felt that I needed to see a professional therapist, which I did for two years. By the time I was 20 I had begun to understand that a large part of my maladjustment was grief, consisting of anger at the felt abandonment at my mother's death and fear that I was not lovable enough that anyone would stay around for me. I slowly began to emerge from my long isolation.

Then, another blow fell on my bruised bones. This pastor, who had so lovingly nurtured me and helped me to begin to have some hope, died in a boating accident, leaving me bereft again. Though I continued to feel a certain spiritual hunger, the notion of a loving God seemed an outright delusion. I sometimes went to church but always sat in the back and did not participate overtly in any way. And so it continued for seven years – through my remaining year of college, my two years of military service and about three years of hippie-style hitch-hiking around Europe and America. I got a job, identified with Becket's morbid humor and the absurdist teaching of Camus, and experimented with drugs and relationships. Looking back on that period, I see that, in a way, I was challenging fate: if I could survive the army, hitching back mountain roads in Montenegro and Greece, wandering the mean streets of American cities till all hours, popping random pills, hanging around with losers, crazies and criminals, perhaps I had a future after all.

However, it was only after I drank the dregs of my self-indulgence that I realized that following my own inclinations would lead me, sooner or later, to jail, madness or death. At that point, at age 27, I said, 'If there's Anybody there, you'd better take over here.' And slowly, over the course of the next five years, I found my way back to my Christian faith and to a religious vocation. Now is not the time to go into all the stages and stories of that journey.

A providential opportunity to work as a volunteer with children who had suffered abandonment and abuse helped me to put my own loss into perspective, and finally to see that my mother's death had prepared me to feel concern for others and to help them search for meaning amidst hardship. My gratitude for the compassion that was growing in me eventually enabled me to forgive God for taking her and allowed me to see that perhaps I had had to go through all that to learn to care about others. After I had been trapped so long in my own misery and self-obsession, I found that simply loving other people was a liberation that made everything that preceded it worthwhile.

Now that long summary is just the background behind the main point I wish to make, which is that a profound childhood experience of loss seems sometimes to be part of the process by which some people find their way to a mature faith and experience a lasting call. A number of spiritual writers, including C.S. Lewis, speak of the mysterious way God sometimes seems to call people through their wounds, their suffering, their weakness. For some of us, God's summons is like a cauterizing touch on an old sore – or perhaps the sore is itself both touch and call. People describe this touch as a burning, a piercing, a being seized. G.M. Hopkins says poignantly, 'Over again I feel thy finger and find thee.'

Among those who were powerfully affected by the early death of a parent we can count C.S. Lewis himself, Thomas Merton, Pope John Paul II, Mother Teresa and many others. Gautama the Buddha was so affected, as was St Anthony of Egypt, father of Christian monasticism, and many later founders, including Ignatius of Loyola and John of the Cross. I have personally known a number of others for whom such a loss irrevocably changed their lives for good or ill.

My hunch is that, when the undergirdings of one's life are rocked and broken by such loss, it causes one to call into question all one's previous certainties, to have radical doubt for all simple solutions, and to seek something solid on which to build life again – some plot of uncluttered earth on which one can, after the earthquake, set up a lean-to and plant a bit of corn. The process varies according to temperament and circumstances. Some people already have the rudiments of a strong faith, others need to search far and wide, experimenting, through trial and error, with various possibilities including wealth, power, pleasure, and fame (as in the Book of Ecclesiastes, which was the only part of the Bible that spoke to me in those years).

After I had engaged in such a search for a number of years, I slowly circled back toward my Christian faith, but with an entirely different perspective from the conventional faith I had learned as a child and rejected as a youth. As with Jacob in Genesis, it was only after I had done my own wrestling with the mysterious stranger that I could look back and say, 'Oh, yes, that must have been the one they were talking about, "the God of our fathers".' The Holy One who waylays prophets and patriarchs is not at first recognizable to them as the God of the tradition.

All the same, as someone who has arrived, after a great loss, at a solid faith in God, how do I know that the one I believe in isn't just some compensatory psychological fantasy, a projection onto blank nothingness of what I have lost, some sort of imaginary friend. I have suspected just that in moments of scepticism and disillusionment. But I habitually test the hypothesis as I would any other. I 'try' the validity of my proposition in various situations – grabbing for it when it might not be there, leaning into it when there is no other support, looking for it behind other apparent solidities.

There is also the person-like evidence – that this Being, whatever it is, seems capable of challenging me in unexpected ways, surprising me into laughter and awe, engaging in a subtle dialogical give-and-take with me, responding to my dilemmas with unpredictable whimsy, trusting me, gracing me with a sense of presence, gratitude, affection. Above all, there is a logical conviction that behind all that exists and apart from everything whatsoever, there is 'What Is' – a 'necessary being', the 'ground of being', that which lends 'is-ness' to every passing thing; that 'No-thing' that 'precedes' and contextualizes the 'big bang' or whatever other cosmogony can be proposed. Perhaps none of that will convince a dyed-in-the-wool sceptic, but it will do for me.

So I am suggesting that people who go through a profound experience of loss often seem to need a surer foundation on which to build their life. They have seen how a life built on sand turns out, and they need to dig down to the bedrock. If this foundation happens to be God, it can touch the heart of a person and move them to want to give themselves to it completely. So, I not only have a relationship with the Absolute, but I know that I could not exist without such a relationship.

How I describe and experience that relationship is a highly personal matter. What disposes me, then, to want to give myself unreservedly to God, to make my bond with the Absolute my defining relationship? Is it, perhaps, at least for some of us, that we cannot trust our poor, broken selves ultimately and utterly to anyone less than God?

It seems that sometimes the pain and the cataclysmic shock of great loss can render a person unable or unwilling to commit totally to any relationship other than one with the Absolute. In the past year or so, I have said to two or three people who know me well: 'I don't think I ever could have married. After all the separations I have suffered, another abandonment, whether through death, sickness, distance or divorce, would just destroy me. I am simply unable to risk it.' It seems almost constitutionally impossible for me to trust myself in an absolute way to anyone but God. I sometimes say, pleading to be understood, 'My Velcro is worn out.' When I shared with these friends this unwillingness to give myself unconditionally to anyone less than God, I expected them to protest, 'Oh, you should face your fears and learn to overcome your insecurities.' But they did not. They understood and accepted what I said at face value. And for me that was a tremendous blessing.

Because, yes, I know, perhaps if I were to go through years of expensive and intensive therapy, I might be able to overcome my fears and marry or make such an unequivocal commitment to another person. But I have found something I value more. In my vocation to the consecrated life as a vowed religious, I have been given a relationship with One who will never abandon me, a relationship that is warm and abiding but that can also vary richly in mood and intensity. Besides, my friendships with many married people over the years convince me that no spouse, no marriage relationship, no matter how intimate, can totally fulfil the infinite need we have for love. Unless both parties in a marriage are grounded in strong loving relationships with friends and with a Higher Power, they risk burdening each other with unrealistic expectations and demands. So even if I were to arrive at a point where I could make such a commitment to another mortal, I would still absolutely need my bond with the one whom I call Way, Truth, Life.

Not only does my vocation give me an opportunity to grow in this foundational relationship with God; it also gives me the reflective time to know myself and process my experiences. And it gives me the occasion to share intimately with numerous others without getting short-circuited into possessiveness and emotional entanglements.

My conclusion is that my mother's death precipitated a process of searching for some sort of lasting truth on which to build my life. That search led me, by a winding road, to a personal faith in God. Then that wound of grief that I could not heal was the very means by which God claimed me, called me and made me his own. Those spiritual writers who speak this way of God as calling us by means of our wounds and weakness, as touching our hearts through our poverty and brokenness, have a wonderful insight. Jesus undermined Peter's impetuous, rock-like stubbornness by one piercing look and claimed his heart forever. Mary Magdalene was done in by her own passionate need and desperate longing. Christ unhorsed Paul, tempering his hot-headed arrogance with temporary blindness and an enduring 'thorn in the flesh'. He captured Francis, the failed troubadour, and Ignatius, the injured warrior. And so on down through the centuries. The doctor who suffers chronic sickness is the charismatic 'wounded healer'. The psychologist who sometimes fears for his own sanity is the gifted therapist. The 'hopeless' alcoholic in recovery is the addiction counsellor who understands to the core those in his charge.

So we could say that sometimes God touches us in a way that wounds us, but the very wound is the invitation, the tap on the shoulder that beckons us to follow, the word of possession that claims us for his own, the grasp of proprietorship that impels us to do the job at hand. Note that I am not making a general statement that things always happen this way. I am only reflecting on my own experience and a pattern that I have noticed in some other lives. The loss that broke my heart for the first time also drove me in the end to seek the One who held the pieces and could forge me a new heart, through fire, turbulence and toil, again and again.

I was talking with a friend a year or so ago, another man who had lost one of his parents at an early age. He suggested that I read Maxine Harris' book, *The Loss That Is Forever*. That book helped me to see that there are many possible responses to the early loss of parents and that my response, though not typical, follows some patterns and makes a certain kind of sense. After all these years, the sore place is still there and can still hurt. Reflecting on all this, I became aware that the thing that seems, at this point, most painful is the fact that my mother did not feel the need to say good-bye, to reassure me of her love or to give me her blessing. That, I think, would have made a tremendous difference. But I take comfort in words that the older of my two sisters wrote to me at the time of my final profession as a religious, when I was 40. She said, 'Mumma would be so proud of you today. She wanted a fourth child so badly and tried for so long before you were conceived. I think she dedicated you to God before you were born.' Perhaps that is blessing enough.

And in any case, now Jesus *is* my heaven, and he is very close, even in my heart. So she is not so far away after all.

5
Seeds from Plastic Flowers

Since I was a little boy accompanying my parents on train trips from our small town in the mountains of Virginia to the big cities of the Eastern Seaboard, it has fascinated me to watch people and how they live their lives. Our train would wend its way past large country mansions with vast lawns, through wealthy suburbs, past cities with glistening banks and towering office buildings, and I would try to imagine what it would be like to live in such places. But what fascinated me far more was when the train passed by shacks with some chickens and a pig and a few bare-footed children, or through the slums with crowded streets and run-down shops, or past grimy factories disgorging hundreds of workers. From our hotel room in Manhattan, I would watch the beggars and winos on the streets below, and the bag ladies with their strange clothes, wandering among businessmen and secretaries and garment factory workers. And on hot summer days we could get glimpses into the tenement buildings nearby, and see whole families getting a little cool air on their fire-escapes.

This interest has continued through my life. My second day as a soldier on assignment in South Korea, taking the train from Seoul south to my new base in Taegu, as we slowly pulled out of the station into the frosty morning haze, I took comfort seeing an elderly woman sweeping out her one-room hut, her breath visible in the icy air. 'If she can endure alone in this cold, hard world, I guess I can survive my tour of duty exiled in this far country.'

Why was I so curious about the lives of the poor? Maybe because I felt poor and lost myself. I still often feel that way, but experience has convinced me that in one sense everybody is poor. The rich are simply those who can afford to hide their poverty from others. (And if they succeed in hiding it even from themselves, they can be a danger to everyone else.)

Toward the end of my fourteenth year, I got a little summer job for the first time and earned some money. Since I had been there so often with my family and knew my way around quite well, I pestered my parents into letting me go to New York City on my own for a week. They had grave doubts (which they probably should have heeded) but finally arranged for me to stay in a reasonably cheap hotel. Its manager was known to my brother, and he agreed to keep an eye on me.

My brother had lived in Manhattan for a couple of years, and on one of our visits had taken my parents and me to an Armenian restaurant. One evening during my week in the city, I located that restaurant and went there for my meal. It was high summer and, as I walked back to my hotel, the streets were full of people escaping the heat and squalor of their tenements. There were drunks and call-girls, soldiers and sailors on leave, neighbourhood families speaking foreign languages, and lots of children. A couple of dogs lay panting on a stoop, and a cat or two cleaned themselves lazily on a wall. A little girl in a thin, soiled dress and no shoes came up to me with a couple of plastic flowers and said, 'Meester, you wanna buy one flower? Is one quarta.' I was flattered because it was the first time anybody had ever called me mister, but I was trying to extend my paltry savings to use for my own pleasures, so I lied, 'I don't have any money.'

Her eyes got big and she said, 'You no money?' I nodded, and she opened her little coin-purse and held it out to me, inviting me to help myself to some of hers. There were only a few coins in it. I mumbled a 'Thanks, that's okay' and hurried shame-facedly up to my room. When I opened the window for some cool air and looked down on the street below, the little girl was still there, going up to passers-by with her two white flowers. But no one was interested.

It was a thought, a wish, not exactly a prayer, but maybe it served as one. 'I'd like to be like that, that confident, that generous, that free.' I wavered for a few moments and then went back down and gave her two dollars for those two plastic carnations. She didn't seem to remember me from a few minutes before and didn't seem surprised at my imagined munificence. I kept those two little carnations for many years, until in a moment of bitterness I threw them away with other signs of a faith which had grown disillusioned at harsher realities. And I forgot the whole incident for many years more.

But even in the years of my bitterness I watched people, little people, and I learned from them. There were times I envied them, even the troubled young man who sat all day every day in a San Francisco Laundromat methodically turning the pages of magazines. At least he had found some way to occupy his time.

It seems God didn't forget what passed as a prayer all those years before, and in his good time decided I was ready to take up this long apprenticeship. Eventually I found the courage to speak to some of the people I was watching and even make friends with them. I tried to follow their example of courage, determination, humility, acceptance, endurance, humour and the many other admirable qualities I saw in them. I also felt their hurt and anger at life's injustices, at society's cruelty, at God's apparent indifference. And yet I felt in my bones the rightness of Jesus' teaching that the poor in spirit are somehow blessed. I have spent much of my adult life trying to understand what that means. I am still trying to understand how to accept my own poverty and how to let God bless me and others through it.

More than 60 years after that summer evening in Manhattan I'm still trying to follow that little girl's example. And when I look back on my years as a kind of monk living and working with people 'on the margins', I am grateful that my teachers – the prisoners, addicts, street people, psychiatric patients, travellers, and others who have befriended me – have been so patient with the slow-learner that I am. I still have hopes that before it comes time for me to discard everything because I won't need it any more, I will have the grace to give it all away, bit by bit, when someone else as poor as I seems to need it more than I.

6
Silence

Every time that I've been back home to Virginia these many years, I've made a pilgrimage to Vesuvius and the summer camp that always meant and still means so much to me. I've walked to Table Rock and Buttermilk Springs and lingered in the outdoor rock chapel: fall, winter, spring, summer. Even now I still dream occasionally that the summer has finally come when I'm free again to pack my old footlocker and go to work in that shady valley. Because it was there, along Big Mary's Creek, that I learned to love the silence – and it is the silence that has led me through all the rich and wrenching moments of my life to this one (also rich and wrenching) – and that I hope will lead me the rest of the way as well.

There's a silence there that's tremendous. And sometimes small sounds make the silence steeper. I think of the sound of cicadas in the hot noon-time, when the dry hush of dust and the heavy stillness of sunlight hold every creature earthbound. And I think of the distant croaking of ravens on high rocks, and the rich repetition of a whippoorwill in the middle of a moonlit night. And young bodies breathing, snoring, sighing in the rustle of sweet straw. And the rush of water over rocks, and the still coolness where water striders skim. Even, from a high ridge the echoed shouts of playing children down below. A stupendous silence, not broken, but accentuated by the small sounds of small creatures. Galactic silences invade that valley, the deep silence of primordial rock creeps up through the soil. The quiet wind steals, touches, troubles water, pine-needles, dead leaves, faded candy wrappers.

We had then what we called the Great Silence. Do they have it still? Strange to impose a monastic rule on hyper-active kids. But somehow, even with the giggles and the guffaws at bed-time, and the poorly-whispered partying of the staff, there was something sacred about that

Great Silence. It got into my blood.

It was there at Camp I learned to love it, and to love the voices, both human and other, that hid within it like crickets in high summer. That silence was pregnant with a presence – of One who can sing with words and notes and melodies, but can sing as well, maybe better, without them.

I don't really need words or photos to remind me of it all. It's still there, somehow, in the silence that has kept me company since those days. Don't forget this, put it on the record once and for all: I am thankful and have not forgotten the friends and fellowship of those years. The first year I came my mother was having treatment for cancer, and by the second summer she had died. Those nine summers at camp were wonderfully healing for me. The love and acceptance I received were balm to a wounded soul, and the silence of the forest calm to a fearful mind. I will not forget that place, or that quiet peace, until the silence that conquers even crickets conquers me, and teaches me too, I hope, to sing without words.

7
On Being Nothing

At times something a friend says helps me see more clearly who I am. I was in Seoul in the Army. I was about 23. The buddies I had lived with the past 10 months were almost all finishing their 13-month tour of duty, which had been extended an extra month because of the North Korean attack on the USS *Pueblo* on 23 January, 1968. We were sitting in our Quonset hut one weekend, drinking beer by the case, and my friends were discussing what they planned to do when they were back in the States. One was going to law school, one into journalism, another into the family clothing business, another into sales. Bradley turned to me and asked, 'Harrison, what are you gonna do when you get out? Be a teacher or something?'

My best friend, Paul, answered as quick as a whip, 'Hell, no, Harrison's not gonna be a teacher! Harrison's not gonna be anything!' Or, it may have been phrased in the poetic vernacular, 'Harrison ain't gonna be nothin'.'

My heart within me quietly shouted 'Yes!' How well Paul knew me! What a good friend he was! It is true that we knew each other well enough to wound each other woefully, sometimes badly enough that we couldn't look each other in the eye for a day or two. But Paul didn't say those words to wound me. They were like an appreciative hug. He knew that I couldn't imagine fitting into any of the usual careers I knew about at that time. He saw clearly that I was a lost soul and would have to search for a way of life that would allow me to be true – to what? – to my uncertainties, to my radical inability to define, limit or pigeon-hole myself. And he knew that I might never find such a way.

Paul's crack was a gentle affirmation of my truth. When we would go out to bars in 'the village' and get very drunk, each of us had, on occasion, propped the other up or even carried the other back to the base to make it in before curfew. We had had long philosophical discussions and shared our youthfully confused hopes and dreams, with the Beatles or Simon and Garfunkle songs playing in the background. The Army was as close to imprisonment as I ever hope to experience, but it gave me the best friends I'd ever had up to that point. And Paul was among the very best. He knew me, accepted me and trusted me. In the five or six years that followed our time together in Korea, we made occasional contact, and I kept Paul up-dated on my ongoing journey.

In those long winter months in Korea, I had done a lot of reading at the base library. One of the books I had come across was Albert Camus' *The Myth of Sisyphus*. It made such an impact on me that I diagrammed its argument, which, if I remember, is approximately as follows. We humans live in a world where we want life, love, goodness and harmony, but we are confronted at every turn with death, fear, evil and discord. If we deny all the good we desire, it is a refusal of our inner truth, a type of suicide. If we deny the reality of the world's woes, it is a refusal of outer actuality, a type of murder. The only way to live the truth and live it fully is to walk the ledge of contradiction, to embrace the absurdity, to ride the crest of the wave where becoming begins its descent into loss.

The first time I read Samuel Beckett's *Waiting for Godot*, I was finishing my last few months of active military duty back in North Carolina and had gone to Washington for a weekend leave. I came across *Godot* in a book-store, bought it, took it back to my hotel and read it through twice without stopping, laughing out loud at its droll depiction of the futile hopes we cling to in a meaningless world. In the years that followed I read most of Beckett's other plays and novels, and many other writers of the absurdist school. A phrase that I came across while reading Jean Genet was 'the road to the ultimate nothingness'. That phrase described the way I saw my path. I knew I was on a metaphysical trajectory, a trek to the end of the world and beyond, into the darkness of the unknowable.

After four years of further exploration of pleasures and disappointments, idleness and work, travels and the settled state, the original sharpness of my way of seeing life's absurdities had shifted a bit. I had begun to realize that the desire for 'nothingness,' my desire to be nobody, was not some life-rejecting nihilism, but a longing to be free from my constant self-scrutinizing, ego-driven self-consciousness. I wanted to find some way of staying permanently in that clear-headed, unselfconscious awareness that came upon me occasionally for a few seconds. But I began to understand that it was virtually impossible to maintain that almost mystical state of open awareness with a mind as flighty and distractible as mine.

I also began to see that to imagine that I could maintain indefinitely that kind of steady clarity of mind demonstrated a kind of grandiosity. In order to escape the pain of my separateness and inner division I was trying to recapture the undifferentiated awareness of womb-life, the paradise-state. I began to realize that it was just such an attempt to co-opt the mind of God that would poison any Eden I might discover. The direction I needed to move in was the opposite of that, toward an actual breaking open of the ego, a reduction of self-centeredness by giving myself to others, a dying to self. I needed to let life break my heart. The nothingness I needed was not like water evaporating upwards to the clouds, but like a rock being eroded downward to soil. Ego, like an egg's shell, is an important defence for the life developing within, but at some point, the shell has to be cracked open and left behind or the result is suffocation and death.

A few months before, I had written a letter to Jeannie, my girlfriend from university days. From my little room in a seedy hotel in San Francisco's night-club district I had described my worries and my struggles to find happiness and meaning in life. She wrote back saying, basically, you are totally self-obsessed and you will never be happy as long as you are focused only on yourself. Those insights prepared me for that life-changing moment hitch-hiking down the Big Sur highway, which I have described in the chapter titled 'Jounrey' abovr. That 'Damascus road' moment landed me at a monastery where I had a few days to reflect on the futility of my journey thus far, and to recognize my need to make some radical changes.

A resolution formed within me to try a different approach, to go with the flow, to let myself be led, to open myself to unforeseen possibilities. I would continue my journey to Mexico and points south as planned but remain open to diversions, digressions and delays. After hoisting my pack over my shoulder and trudging down from the monastery to resume my southward travel along the Pacific Coast Highway, I came across a man changing a flat tyre. This was my first opportunity to do something different, to help somebody, to give. We wrestled the new tyre into place and tightened the lug nuts. He gave me a lift to Santa Barbara. I was on my way.

During the week I spent in Santa Barbara I met the director of a home for abandoned and abused children placed by the courts. Listening to him talk about the kids he worked with, and his recent visit to one of them in the juvenile prison, my heart was moved, and I thought, perhaps this is something I am supposed to do. I asked if I could stop by this 'ranch' for a few weeks before continuing my journey. The staff kept me busy with little errands and maintenance jobs, and the kids delighted me with their disarming playfulness and trust.

After that brief experience of usefulness and community, I carried on with my travel plans. But after about a month on the road I decided, or rather let chance decide for me, to cut short my Latin American journey at Patzcuaro, in central Mexico. I found myself taking a series of buses back to the 'ranch'. I had soon realized that if I was going to be open to the promptings of my heart, I belonged with those kids, not on the lonely road to Tierra del Fuego. I arrived in town in the middle of the night, took a room in a motel, and phoned my director friend the next morning to see if I would be welcome as a long-term volunteer.

I worked for the next five years as a yardman, delivery driver, poolcleaner, errand-runner, and general maintenance guy at that home for kids placed by the courts because of abuse, neglect or other problems. 'The ranch' was in a small town in the Mojave Desert. As a volunteer I had the time and freedom to think things over, to hike out in the rugged red- and black-rock mountains, to explore the deep shadowed ravines leading down to the Colorado River, to take shelter in shallow caves from the rock-baking heat of the desert sun. Working with religious people, and acting as an older brother to those tough kids, gave me an opportunity to review the trajectory of my life thus far, to see what were the major lessons I had learned, and to reflect on the direction my wandering way would take next. In those early months at the ranch I was still not sure whether I could say that I believed in anything much. I was leery of the word 'God'. But I was already experiencing some kind of presence or inner prompting, a sense of companionship, a feeling that there was something, someone, beside me or somewhere near me on my lonely way.

I started reading the Gospels from a different angle, looking upon Jesus as a teacher of a certain kind of visionary mystical wisdom that might have the capacity of liberating me from the traps of self, social conformity, and fear, and of opening me to a radical serenity. I came up with two short precepts that helped me move forward toward that freedom that was so appealing to me:

'Look through all things to the Whatever beyond.'
'Withhold nothing.'

'Whatever' was, for some months, my name for God. Those two precepts were as close as I could get, at that time, to Jesus' summary of the law – to love God and neighbour. If I was going to pursue the freedom of becoming that very concrete 'nothing' that my friend Paul had prophesied, then I would have to search for that oneness, that principle of is-ness, lying at the heart of, or beyond the appearance of, the ten thousand things. And I would have to submit myself to the process of diminishment, change and loss that would reduce me from the knot of self-obsession and conflicting desires that I then was toward that simpler, cleaner acceptance of myself as a small creature in a vast universe. I would have to relinquish the grandiose notion of becoming some purely spiritualized nothing, and content myself with being in the process of flesh and blood self-emptying modeled by Jesus in his life of service and sacrifice.

Thus I continued my experiment of trying to live more for others. After this process had been working its magic in me for a couple of years, Paul paid me a short visit at the ranch on his way from Florida to California. It was the summer holiday, and I drove with Paul and a van full of kids down to Kingman Wash, a cove on the Arizona side of Lake Mead. After a couple of hours swimming in the lake, diving off the rocks and baking in the desert heat, as we drove back to the ranch with the wind in our hair, loud music on the radio, and the kids laughing in the back, Paul looked at me with affection and a bit of envy and said, 'Whatever you've found, man, whatever you call this, make sure you keep hold of it.' The next morning, unshaven and a bit hung over, he loaded his car and continued his journey. I don't know what happened to him after that. We lost contact.

But those words Paul spoke about me that day in Seoul have echoed through the years. I told the story to the Dominican priest who received me into the Catholic Church when I was 30, and he understood the humour and the challenge of my call to be nothing and has reminded me of it several times since then. As I was approaching my perpetual vows as a brother at age 40 I had been considering conflicting possibilities for the future. Feeling the need for some clarity, I prayed that God would give me 'a word', an image that would be like a compass reading for my continuing journey. Over the months following that prayer I kept remembering Paul's comment and other similar nudges that I had felt over the years to shed my masks and delusions, to unburden myself of roles and routines, to become little, to vanish, to be free – free of self, free to give all that a little soul can give.

That is the 'word' that calls me still. Moving into that freedom is not a destination, not even a process. It is just *this* next step into the unknown, *this* act of giving what I cannot spare, *this* choice to take the risk to love. I still feel my self as the greatest encumbrance on my journey home. The way is unending, and sometimes it seems I have hardly begun. Over the years, however, I have learned this much:

> The goal is the heights, but the way is down.
> The goal is the stars, but the path is in.
> The goal is the light, but the road is dark.

And I pray to the one who emptied himself utterly and was broken open for me, to get me through that needle's eye, that nadir, that nil point, until what's left of me is a pile of grit and a song of praise. Amen.

8

A Dangerous Gift

We need to jump back briefly, now, to the time after my Army days but before I ended up at the Ranch. Although for a number of years I considered myself a non-believer, at age 26 I was still aware of a spiritual hunger and open to trying various ways to fill it. I had long wanted to spend some time in a monastery and, during the period of my hitch-hiking travels around North America, I arranged to spend a month at a monastery of Anglican monks on the Hudson River in up-state New York.

It was a good month. I helped out with various chores, especially in the kitchen, the garden and the grounds, talked with the monks and attended some of the liturgies, during which I carefully avoided anything that I considered participation. I could join in the work and community life of the monks, but when it came to prayer, I was strictly an observer. Toward the end of the month, I asked to have a chat with the Prior. I told him that I really liked their contemplative lifestyle but didn't believe in God or the Christian view of things. He said, 'Well, the whole point of our way of life is to lead us to a deeper relationship with God, so if you don't believe, there would be no point in living here.'

'But,' he went on to say, 'don't forget that faith is a gift.'

'Right,' I said. 'That makes sense. I don't have that gift.'

The Prior continued, 'But, if you want it, you could always ask for it.'

'Ask whom? If I don't believe, who would I be asking for it?' I grinned. 'Or is that some kind of a little trick to predispose me toward faith?'

He looked at me piercingly, as though asking, 'And are you predisposed *not* to believe?' Within myself I had to admit, eventually, that I was. I was angry at the hurts life had dealt me, the abandonments I had suffered, the limitations I encountered in myself, and the faults I found with the world. I was afraid to set myself up for more painful disappointments. I didn't want to fall for the pretty dreams the preachers peddled, and I didn't want to become one of those obnoxious Jesus-junkies or self-righteous morality merchants. To be honest, I wanted to carry on as I was, chasing pleasures that were considered sinful by those with faith. So, I put all the Prior's words out of my mind for the moment.

But he had planted a seed. I slowly began to understand that faith was not something I could manufacture or muster up on my own. If I had none, I could ask for it. If I already had it in a latent form, I could ask to stop denying it. Ask who? That wasn't clear. The life-force that had kept me alive through various dangers? The deeper truth that I was always looking for, beyond surface appearances? The hope for some kind of ultimate meaning?

In any case, it was clear from my talk with the Prior that I couldn't stay longer at the monastery, so I packed my kit, said my farewells and prepared to leave the next morning. Another visitor was also leaving, and offered to give me a lift as far as Chicago. I had 28 cents to my name, though a friend from college arrived that evening and slipped me a 10-dollar bill for the journey.

We spent one night in the parking lot of a Salvation Army shelter somewhere in Ontario, then on across Michigan to the outskirts of Chicago. The next day it was across Iowa in heavy football traffic, and along the Platte River Valley through Nebraska. The following day I made it half-way across Colorado and slept in the back seat of the car at a young construction worker's house in Denver. The next morning, he was going up into the mountains, where he let me out just in time to receive a no-hitch-hiking warning from the Colorado Highway Patrol. But then another young guy gave me a lift down through the red-rock desert side of the Rockies to Grand Junction, entrusting to me a ring to give to his girlfriend Louise if I came across her in San Francisco.

After a short wait, a cluttered, dusty old station wagon with a hippie couple and a dog came to a gliding halt and waited for me to catch up. They were going all the way to Oakland (California). But that first night we ended up in the mountains of Utah, blocked by a snow-bank, and had to retrace our route 100 miles and go around by a lower pass. We must have slept in the car that night, and maybe the next as well as we made our way across Nevada from Ely to Reno and down into the Central Valley of California.

When I finally got back to San Francisco after that journey, I found it hard to return to my former indigence. One evening sitting innocently in front of City Hall, I was attacked, unprovoked, by somebody who, I suppose, didn't like long-haired hippies. So, I decided to get off the streets and find some stability. I went to a job centre, where they offered to send me for an interview with a freight-forwarding company. I had the weekend to do the round of charity shops and find some decent clothes. But I was worried how I would wake up in time for the interview. I was used to sleeping till mid-day, was staying in a seedy hotel with a window that faced a brick wall, and I had no clock. My buddy was inside a shop phoning his girlfriend to see if we could come by to use her iron to press my second-hand shirt, and I was standing outside on Market Street waiting. As dozens of pedestrians passed by, one old man, probably alcoholic, held out his closed hand to me, and I responded with my open palm. There it was, right in my hand, a pocket watch, ticking, the correct time. It wasn't an alarm clock, but it would serve the purpose. Amazed, I looked up to see who it had been, but he was already lost in the crowd. I knew I would get that job.

My work consisted in making arrangements for people who had anything from a few pieces of luggage up to a household full of furniture (or possibly just a new refrigerator or a luxury car) to have their belongings packed, moved from their home, held in storage for a designated time if necessary, then shipped overseas, to be delivered to an inland destination and unpacked. Part of this process was the customs documentation, which was minimal, but for which we charged a hefty fee.

At one point I had a phone call from a Catholic medical missionary nun. She and two of her fellow sisters were being assigned to work in an orphanage in Taiwan, and each of them had one footlocker of personal effects to ship. We had a lively chat on the phone, and she seemed a pleasant, up-beat sort. I offered to put all three trunks on the one bill of lading and to charge her only one documentation fee. It wasn't really as generous as she thought, since she could easily have filled the form out herself in a few minutes and taken it to be stamped at the Customs House. But we were the experts and she was happy to let us do it.

About six months later I received a letter from her from Taiwan, informing me that all three trunks had arrived by ship, safe and sound. She thanked me for my kindness and assured me that she had all her orphans praying for me. I have come to wonder how much those prayers influenced the course of my life after that. At the time I thought nothing of it, but looking back years later, I wonder if those prayers had anything to do with the chain of events that led me from the confusion of my wandering days to the volunteer work, into which I stumbled a year or two later, with abused and neglected children, and beyond that, into a whole different way of life.

Now, many years later, after I have covered thousands more miles on my own journey of faith, I often meet young people searching for a way forward out of addiction, criminality, unemployment and depression. Many people in the early months of AA or NA are completely confused by the notion of spirituality and what recovery programs refer to as a Higher Power.

I often repeat to them the conversation I had with the Prior at West Park all those years ago. Everyone seems to understand the notion that faith isn't something we can produce on our own or even wish into being. They understand that faith is something added, something a person has to be given, or perhaps, better, gifted with. But the thought that you might consider asking for it is another matter. People look at me with their arms crossed, just as I did at the Prior. Asking for the gift might just predispose me to be open to it if it comes. Praying for it could make me susceptible to the dangerous gift of faith. But then the question arises, am I predisposed not to believe?

Is our ingrained suspicion and scepticism regarding spiritual realities a natural reticence, or have we been conditioned to defend ourselves from credulity? There are, I have to admit, good reasons to be defensive. First, because there are so many people peddling suspect goods and counterfeit escape tickets. And, second, because the real thing is probably even more dangerous than the spurious alternatives.

Make no mistake, trust is a risk. I often think that people who react with fear to the very mention of God are right. They have every reason to be afraid – terrified, in fact. Faith can really change your life

– beyond all recognition. The Bible is full of stories of people whose lives were radically redirected when they opened themselves to the gift of faith. And faith begins very small, seeps through our defences like water through cracks in cement. I'm not even sure I ever actually asked for it. Perhaps I only stopped resisting it. At first it might just be faith that life is worth the struggle, or that there are a few decent people around, or that I might have a future after all. As we go with the flow, faith grows and with it hope, and then we may be able to see and understand things that didn't make sense before.

When we reach a point of actually praying, things can really take off. But prayer of a certain kind! When I pray God to fix my problems or clean up my messes so that I can go on with life as usual, nothing seems to happen. When I am desperate and open to anything, ready to let 'demolition precede reconstruction', then things start changing. If I ask for the courage to face some obstacle or the humility to admit some fault, and then I find I'm given the virtue I asked for, my faith begins to send out tendrils. As I test the ice to see if it will hold my weight, I get the courage to venture further out from land. I watch people struggling to make sense of all this, and I see amazing transformations unfold before my eyes.

I had been ready to risk my life on many dubious highs and cheap thrills that brought me fleeting happiness or none at all, before I was ready to risk it on what has brought me increasing freedom, joy, and peace. Yes, there have been loneliness and heart-break along the way. But I have come to understand that loneliness is the limitless longing for unlimited love, and heart-break enlarges the soul to contain the fullness of God's peace.

A hymn I learned at university says it well:

> ... such happy, simple fisher-folk, ...
> before they ever knew
> the peace of God that filled their hearts
> brimful, and broke them too....
>
> The peace of God, it is no peace,
> but strife closed in the sod.

> Yet let us pray for but one thing—
> the marvellous peace of God.
>
> William A. Percy, 'They cast their nets in Galilee'

For the fact is, once I had been given a modicum of faith, I found myself trying it out in new situations, found myself reading about others who had been drawn by faith to attempt amazing adventures and explore hopes and dreams that led them to the heights of freedom and self-giving: people like the Desert Fathers, like St Benedict and St Francis, like Charles de Foucauld, like Thomas Merton and Mother Teresa. I read the works of classic and modern spiritual writers, developing a stronger appetite for the contemplative spirituality that had attracted me to that New York monastery in the first place. I had met people who had committed themselves to lives oriented by their convictions, and I had spent many hours in the solitude of desert and mountains, of churches and chapels, and, step by step, faith had led me to a deep desire to give myself more fully to God and to find the freedom of dancing the dance of his will for me.

Eventually I discovered in myself the courage to actually 'try my vocation', to see if I was cut out for some sort of monastic or religious life, a life vowed totally to God. And, even more surprising, I found that that kind of life suited me well, though it was far from easy. I know myself to be a man without much courage, and one with a very low pain threshold, and I have grave doubts about my ability to withstand much suffering, physical, emotional, or spiritual. Even knowing that, the gift of faith has pushed me to dare God to work a miracle and make me faithful, despite myself, to the desire he placed in my heart all those years ago, the desire to be his man.

I hope that, by some fluke, I will manage to live up to the desire I expressed at age 40 when I tried to explain to my friends and family what I was doing in making my perpetual profession as a religious brother, a kind of Christian monk. This was my explanation back then:

> Some of you may wonder what this means, 'final profession of vows.'
>
> Final means forever. To profess something means to proclaim

it, to make a public act of faith. Vows are solemn promises that bind.

What I am doing June 29 is a wild, crazy gesture of love – it's binding myself to God for all time – it's an impossible act of faith.

It's like Peter when he said, 'Lord, I will die for you!' He believed it, he meant it. And we all know he failed. He soon denied Jesus, and the cock crowed. But a little later Jesus gave him a chance to repent and to proclaim, 'I love you, I love you. Lord, you know I love you!' And in the long run, Peter's protests of love came true, and his promise to die for Jesus came true too. Maybe the fact that he was fool enough to say it helped it happen.

So I'm undertaking to live a poor, chaste, obedient life among the poor. Why? Because that's the kind of life Jesus lived on earth, and I want to (need to) follow him as close as I can. I've been lost in the dark before, and I hope never to be lost again. That means I've got to stay right close to Jesus and share the circumstances of his life, because he's the only one who knows where I am. He's my life. Without him I'm dead and done for. If he didn't love me, I would never have been born. And so to love him is life for me.

Do you understand any better now than you did before? If not, that's ok. Because really, vocation is a mystery, a secret between a person and his God. And Love has been known to make a man do funny things. Just pray I'm faithful to the Love that calls me and draws me and drives me to this extremity!

Forty-five years later I am still walking in the company of my Lord, 'my friend indeed'. I haven't found a better companion or a more faithful friend. As in any friendship, there are days that we don't see eye to eye, days when we don't even speak to each other. But I still pray that he will continue to give me, day by day, the gift of faith and the desire to belong to him, heart and soul. At one point, the year before I made that final profession, when it came time to renew my vows for another year, I was praying in the sub-basement chapel of a Los Angeles sky-scraper and realized that I didn't know what I believed or whether I could commit myself to such an uncertain future. I finally decided that I could commit myself to the Truth, whatever that might be, and let the Truth, the deepest, most enduring Truth, whatever that might be (even if it were an emptiness, a void, a total lack of meaning), work on me and in me in whatever way it would. This is what I take John the gospel-writer to mean by 'consecration in the truth'.

As it turns out, I came to understand more deeply that Jesus *is* the Truth. He is also the Way on which I journey into the fullness of Truth, and the Life that animates my days on my voyage toward the fullness of Love. The joy that I anticipate is the joy of freedom from myself, freedom to love, and to give myself and my all to the One who gives himself unreservedly to me. Walk with me always, Lord. 'I have faith. Lord, help my lack of faith!'

9
Gazing into Night

Reading certain words the other day abruptly re-constellated for me the feelings of a very dark period of my life. It was when I was just emerging from a time of youthful searching, of trying to orchestrate experiences that would make my life endurable. In that pursuit I had fallen into moral traps, addictions, and depression, and I was just at the point of realizing that I was chasing fantasies, that my illusions were leading me into dangerous waters, and that as long as I continued to pursue beguiling dreams, I would have to navigate veritable nightmares.

Though I always had a philosophical bent, I had little idea of what the truth was, scant understanding of reality. The whole vast human social enterprise seemed to be based on deceptions and pretences as transparent as my own. Yet I knew that I wanted to live in reality, whatever it was, and not to lose myself irretrievably in the pursuit of my imaginary improvements on the facts. I needed to touch the cold, jagged rocks of real walls. I needed to feel the sharp, rugged bark of actual trees. The truth, even if it was painful and disappointing, was safer than the falsehoods I had been feeding on. Better to eat dry bread softened with the spit of my mouth than to go hungry dreaming of banquets.

So these words from the Psalms, when we said them yet again the other day, took me back to the raw relief of those early days of learning to accept, or better, to embrace, the real:

> Our life is over like a sigh.
> Our span is seventy years,
> or eighty for those who are strong.
> And most of these are emptiness and pain.
> They pass swiftly and we are gone. (Psalm 89, Grail)

That is not how I experience life now, nor in fact have I experienced it thus for a long time. But there was a lengthy stretch, amounting to several years, that I crossed each day off my calendar when it was done as a chore accomplished, one more instalment of a large mortgage paid, one more increment of a life-sentence served, and the sooner done the better.

I didn't know if there was any meaning to life. I strongly suspected there was not and had so suspected for a long time. That had been my justification for the pursuit of pleasure: if nothing matters, let's at least enjoy what we can. But enjoyment as self-indulgence had left a bitter after-taste and had led me down that very primrose path that I had just abandoned in dismay. No, I resolved to sit and look squarely into the emptiness, the darkness, the dullness of that moonless night until I could tell whether there was any meaning there, any point to it all – or not. I would wait as long as necessary. I would tolerate the deprivation as long as I could. And then I would know what to do with my days, whether to endure the drudgery, how to fill the tedium of the intervening years until the descent of merciful oblivion.

At that time, I was staying in a small town in the Mojave Desert, and when I wasn't doing the work I needed to feed and shelter myself, I had the time to take long walks out into the black- and red-rock hills, to hike down the dry washes and steep ravines carved by occasional flash-floods, or to dive off cliffs into Lake Mead or Lake Mojave and swim out to a cove where I'd not see another soul the whole day long. The only evidence of prior human visitation might be rusted tin cans around an abandoned miner's shack, or the tracks left by some off-road vehicle and a few spent shotgun shells. In the glare of midday, I could shelter in the shack, or in the shadow of a cliff, or in a shallow cave, always checking first for scorpions and rattlesnakes. And at night there was usually a vast, clear sky in its silent array, but with the sounds of small movements close by and, in the middle distance, the periodic yelping of coyotes.

It was as though I sat and gazed into metaphysical nothingness, like an astronomer at this telescope on a foggy night, waiting for the clouds to lift. And at one point I see a flash of light and then realize it is low lamplight reflected in the telescopic lens from my own eye. But as I sit and my heart grows still and my breath grows long – I speak here not of moments but of months – I begin, not to see, but to know that there is a reciprocating stillness and another waiting that is alert to mine.

It is not a mere projection, a reflection of my 'I'. It is vast and quiet. It is as close to me as my breath, and, at the same time, as the clouds disperse, it is farther than the farthest points of light at the lead edge of the cosmic tsunami. And though this desert night is cold, and though the interstellar night is far colder still, I feel warmth. I can't focus on anything sure, I can't hear any single sound, but I discern a presence, and I know that one is there – one that speaks by silence and sees eyeless from within – one who – oh, what's the use? I can't describe it. It is an 'I'. And it is a 'You'. And it is Love. And it unleashes in my soul a whirling dance of pure, free joy. And it causes to surge up in me a song that splits my heart in splinters of gladness. And what's the use? I can't describe it.

I would like, once for all, to fight past the darkness of my own blinding self-absorption, beyond the tides of my deluded dreams and my despair. I long to surge through the hauling riptides of our futile human complacencies, past the kelp-beds of society's narcissistic snaring ropes of thrall. I still hope to lose myself in the immensity of that night sky, travel out beyond the breakers that heave against the invisible sandbars of our Milky Way, on into the vast open sea of space to distant stellar reefs and atolls, toward ultimate horizons, beyond which that One also abides who, I know, is with me here and now.

In the daytime you can see things meters or miles away, but in this night, you can see light-years. And as dawn rises, I discern my empty coffee cup and my dusty glasses case and the breviary open to Psalm 89. 'And most of these are emptiness and pain.' Ah, but what an emptiness! An emptiness full, if only I could see, of You! And pain, sweet heart-break, that delivers me from me.

Is there a meaning to my life? Only one. You. Oh, and yes, there's also the joyful love that you release in us like cold, clear water from a desert spring. What more is there to say? Nothing, really. Nothing. Let it be.

10

Man of the Road

In my wandering days, before God led me to the place he made for me, I was once hitch-hiking from the San Francisco Bay Area to Southern Nevada. I had enough money for bus-fare to Santa Maria and then hitched back roads to the monastery at Valyermo, where I had arranged to take refuge for a few days on my way home.

In that period a succession of broken souls found a temporary home at the monastery, and there was one such man there in those months. I don't know whether the Prior, Fr John, brought these men from the veterans' hospital where he did some work in the psychiatric wards, or whether they just gravitated to St Andrew's as leaves drift to a peaceful eddy in a stream. In any case, this particular man was very quiet. He helped in the kitchen and with the grounds and attended Mass and the Offices with silent devotion. He had the weathered look of a hobo and the puffy eyes of a chronic alcoholic, although he was evidently sober and at peace in the safe haven of the Priory. He was probably more at peace than I. I was still fairly young, but I could see that if I continued my wandering ways for long, I could easily end up weary and battered like him, in his worn-out khakis and his disintegrating flight jacket.

One evening at dusk I strolled along the old entry road that lay between two rows of cottonwoods and forded the creek, curving up to Pallet Creek Road. My mind was full of uncertainties, temptations, warring thoughts. As I reached the paved road, which was still warm from the afternoon sun, part of me yearned to just keep walking, lured by the fleshpots of the big city lying just the other side of the mountains. I could practically feel the hum of that sprawling expanse of humanity, the pull of the various ways I could lose myself there, could find release, oblivion, shipwreck. Another part of me just wanted to head off into the desert, to find some cave or gully where I could, like Elijah, give in to my despair and perhaps, on the morrow, be fed by ravens and set a task by an angel from God. But dark had fallen, night's stillness was settling in and the stars were beginning to show. I turned back toward the retreat house, kicking up dust. The battle for my future was left unresolved once more, and the thought of my bed drew me toward the uneasy truce of sleep.

As I dragged my steps wearily past the refectory, I could see the light on in the kitchen. At that time the kitchen windows were still clear, not opaque as now, and I could see the little tramp alone inside. He had just finished the mopping, and he stood there for a few moments, surveying the counters, the stoves, the work-tables. Everything was in order, all the utensils in their drawers, all the surfaces tidy. He stood still for another moment, then quietly, reverently genuflected, went slowly to the door, turned off the lights and left.

His action woke me with a start from my headful of thoughts, fantasies, fears and worries. God is truly here, palpably present in this very place, in this very moment. Christ is truly present in the kitchen, breathingly alive here where I stand outside, as the quail make their little night noises beneath the junipers. To genuflect, to bend the knee, is to proclaim one's faith that God becomes flesh in Jesus, abides with us tenderly in the Eucharist. But my little hobo finds him truly present in the empty scullery, feels him heart-breakingly near amid the quiet clicking of the ovens as they cool. It doesn't matter what tomorrow brings, the Holy One is here, now. That's all I need. Like my fellow wanderer, I am at peace. Whatever tomorrow brings, wherever the road leads, God is there. All days and all roads are encompassed in this moment in this desert night. Emmanuel, God-with-u-s, is evoked, recognized and adored in the humblest gesture of the least of his brothers. I am the witness, and for a moment I understand, I see.

11

Musings of a Wannabe Monk

I woke up from my desert siesta sweating. I had just struggled up from a dream in which I was weeping and calling out, 'I want to be a monk.' That was back when I was first beginning to think about religious life. After visiting a number of orders, it became clear that my vocation was to be a brother in an active order. But, 40 some years later, I have never stopped feeling that on some deep level God calls me still to be 'a monk'. Whenever the desire to run away to the cloister has been strong, I have learned to read it as God's way of telling me to live the gift of my present commitment more contemplatively. There is something archetypal about the image of the monk – something that speaks deeply to my heart about ultimate values.

When I was a young brother in Los Angeles, we used to come occasionally to Valyermo, this monastery in the high desert an hour and a half drive north of the city, for retreats, sometimes just for a day, sometimes for a few days, sometimes for a week or more. On more than one of those occasions, one of the monks, Fr Gregory, said to me, 'We love it when you brothers come up because you expect us to be monks.' When I was appointed novice director, Fr Francis gave me a copy of the Desert Fathers stories, knowing that their style appealed both to my bare-bones spirituality and my droll humor. Even now, when I spend time at a monastery, I almost always leave reluctantly, carrying a sort of anticipated homesickness. I know that it would be very different living monastic life every day, and I don't doubt that God has me where he wants me, but the longing is still powerful.

Over the years, when men in prison, students in schools where I have given talks, or people enquiring about our work with the poor, have asked me, 'What are you, some kind of priest or what?', I have found the easiest response is, 'Oh, I'm sort of a half-baked monk.' True, our vocation is much more than that, but that's a good starting place and one that people readily grasp.

So the question I ask myself now is, what does this image represent for me? And is there some way I can appropriate some of its meaning in my actual vocation?

For me the monk is a man who is committed in an absolute manner to the Absolute. The word monk comes from *monachos*, 'alone or single', from *monos,* 'one'. The monk's call is to be one with the One, single-hearted in seeking the one thing worth everything – also to be one with humankind in its sin and in its saving; one with nature, surrounding him with its colours, forms and seasons; and one with himself, trying to bring into harmony within himself all the contrasting strivings of his human heart. The solitary aspect of his journey is countered by the one-ing with others in community life and the Church – leading to a certain uniformity in simplicity, based on the knowledge that we have much more in common than we have different, and that even our idiosyncracies, eccentricities, and foibles are predictably human.

Theoria is Greek for beholding or contemplating, and the contemplative life seems to me 'theoretically' sound. It is a life founded on the premise that He Who Is wants us to be totally one with him in his triune way – Living, Knowing and Loving, the activities that quintessentially comprise his Being. In the time of my vocational searching, I carried in my wallet a phrase from Psalm 27 – 'One thing I ask of the Lord, one thing I seek – to live in the house of the Lord all the days of my life, to behold the sweetness of the Lord and to consult him in his temple.' Of course, there are many ways one can dwell in the precincts, but 'theoretically', the monastic life accomplishes it with unequivocal clarity. The temple is the sacred area measured off for the worship of the Holy, and to dwell within the temple is con-temple-ation. Monasticism is a measured way of life that gives priority of space and time to God present with us here and now.

What else appeals to me about the life of the monk? Silence, solitude, simplicity. I remember once, when travelling from Sicily to Paris, I had a couple of hours between trains in Rome. I took the bus to St Peter's Basilica and went into the Blessed Sacrament Chapel, with its high velvet curtains hushing out the comings and goings in the busy nave.

That huge Baroque altar with its enormous tabernacle and embellishments, the gathering of people from all over the world singing *Tantum ergo*, the towering monstrance with its golden rays and the decorative medallions around its base, were all focused on the shocking poverty of a circle of minimalist bread which was, moreover, emptied of its breadly substance to make way for the One who emptied himself to the point of nothingness – a oneness impinging on naught, a nothingness filled with a Reality so vast as to be unthinkable. The whole vast architectural and hierarchical structure of the Church is there only at the service of and to provide the context for that utterly simple, silent, solitary Presence – the One who became poor to break bread with the poor, who gave himself utterly in loving obedience, in faithful attendance on the hoped-for bride.

The monk is one who leaves the trappings behind and ventures into the emptiness, the contradiction, the cloud, the darkness of the Holy of Holies in search of that Presence whose tender waiting there melts his heart, releases his tears, and allows him to forget himself at last.

There is so much more. The monk is the man of desert wastes and mountain wilderness; whose life is praise, is song, is quiet exultation; who is neither surprised nor afraid at his own misery and unfaithfulness; who doesn't mind dirty jobs; whose spirit finds nourishment in fasts; whose soul is moved by the night's deep stillness; who can laugh with brothers and smile at strangers; who can look into all things and sense Someone humbly waiting; who can hear conviction in the wind and take comfort in the croaking of the frogs. Yes, it's all so romantic, so idealistic. But that is what archetypes are for: they embody a truth that speaks to our heart. And for me the truth that 'the monk' speaks is this: 'Live your life in quiet confidence that God is All in all and you are almost nothing; his essence is love and that love will win you. That's all, absolutely all, you need to know.'

Those of you who are 'the real thing', don't worry. We know you can't live up to all that we project on you. We accept you and love you with and even because of your weaknesses and lack of congruence. After all, our broken Saviour reveals the paradox that the most fitting witness to the One Who Is is one whose 'name is an oil poured out'

(Song of Songs 1:3), poised on the point of vanishing. We pray that you may more and more live up to what your vocation means to you – but we ask your prayers that we, your wannabe brothers and sisters, may claim in our own lives the stupendous gifts that your vocation symbolizes so forcefully for us. You hold the treasure in your hands, but you hold it for us too.

12
Seeing Light

Sitting by the lilac bushes at the desert monastery, I was gazing out past the row of young poplars, across the little pasture with its white fence, toward the eroded desert hillside above Pallet Creek Road. As I relaxed my focus, it struck me that I was seeing only one thing. I was seeing light. The same light that was fluttering brightly in the cottonwood leaves was soaking into the pale bark of the tree trunks, was reflected by the white fence boards, and was casting shadows of ridges and culverts and juniper bushes on the distant slopes. For those few moments, I didn't see all those things. I saw only one thing – the light.

I'm not sure whether that was before or after I first heard of a nun who worked with the poor in Calcutta. When that happened, I was 27 and had accompanied a group of kids to a church camp in the Sierras by Lake Tahoe. For some reason, when I think of that occasion I remember standing on a sunny slope, looking past ponderosa pines toward the icy, glimmering lake and the mountains beyond, the one light reflected on many surfaces. That was the moment when someone told me that we were going to watch a film that evening, about this woman called Mother Teresa. It was Malcolm Muggeridge's famous television documentary called *Something Beautiful for God*, which was later made into a book with the same title.

I was just beginning to crawl back to the faith after some years of looking for happiness without it, and I was surprised to see somebody trying to live Christian values to the full. St Francis had always appealed to me, even when I was sceptical of religion. But here was a contemporary of my own, living a radically simple life according to the program described in the Gospels, which I was beginning to suspect might be worth re-examining. Following my own will, living for my selfish pleasures certainly hadn't proved a satisfactory or satisfying way to organize my life. Maybe this ancient wisdom of living according to noble principles, for the good of others, might have something to offer.

This is not the time to speak of the steps and stages of that exploration. But I began to read a lot of spiritual books. I came across something that helped me over several hurdles. I think it was in a book by Evelyn Underhill, though I haven't been able to relocate the text. The passage was speaking of Eucharistic adoration, and it said something to the effect that what Catholics were adoring in Eucharistic worship was not so much the Consecrated Host in its own right, even as the Bread of Life. Rather they were seeking to gaze through the 'accidents' of the host into the mystery of the Incarnate Word, and beyond even that, into the ineffable glory of the Godhead. I understood that Jesus, the Eternal Word, came to be with us in the Host, as he had been with us in the flesh, precisely in order to allow us to look through him, beyond him, into the deep heart of the Unknowable, the Invisible God, the One who dwells in unapproachable light.

It seems to me that this dynamic of seeing through and looking beyond is a pattern that permeates our faith. When I saw that film and later read some books about Mother Teresa, I could see that she never wanted to be the centre of attention but was always pointing away from herself toward Jesus, who had said to her, 'Come, be my light.' 'We do it for Jesus', a frequent expression of hers, was used as the title of a book of her insights. She would ask newly arriving sisters why they had come, and if they said it was to serve the poor, or to be a missionary, or to follow her example, she would say, 'Then, pack your bags and go home. The only reason to be here is to belong to Jesus.'

When she received the Nobel Prize, she specifically stated that she accepted it on behalf of the world's poor. And she always spoke at length about the goodness, the kindness, the generosity of the poor whom she served, removing the focus from her own work and directing it toward them. And even in that ministry for the poor, while loving and respecting the person before her, she could also look into and beyond that person and see Jesus, her spouse, in the distressing disguise of that suffering soul who stood before her.

We can detect the same process in the Gospels. Jesus is always trying to get people to look beyond his miracles and his teaching and to see his loving, merciful Father. The Father, in his turn, directs our attention away from himself when he says, 'This is my beloved Son, listen to him.' (Mark 9:7) Christ bears witness to the Spirit, who will lead us into the fullness of truth, but we only recognize the Spirit when he moves our hearts, prompting us to call God 'Abba' and to acknowledge Christ as Saviour. The Holy Spirit often seems to be the most diffident and elusive of all, and likes to hide himself in the most unlikely places, even in our hearts, or in the words of those we call our enemies.

On one occasion, our Lord assures his disciples that they will do even more marvellous things than he, in effect saying that he would yield the spotlight to them. In his last moments of earthly life, Our Lord directs our attention toward his Mother, and hers toward the Beloved Disciple when he says, 'Behold your son.' Each one is always refusing to be the center of attention and asking us to seek deeper into the mystery of the other.

All this does not mean that we are not to look with the eyes of faith at our Lord or at our Lady, or to try to train our attention toward the Spirit, toward God himself. In fact, we are to be captivated by their beauty, but their beauty always reflects and directs our gaze to the others and to the depths. In seeing everything, we see one thing, the Light.

Some Christians are jealous on God's behalf when people honour the saints and angels, feeling that these lesser figures are distracting us from giving the full glory due to God. But the reflections sparkling on the surface of the lake, the glint of mica and quartz facets in the granite boulder, and the shimmering of sunlight on poplar leaves and pine needles all reflect and magnify the glory of sun and invite us to look beyond the forms, to lift our eyes to the heights, to rest our gaze, not on the sun itself, but on the deep vault of heaven. The 100 prisms of a chandelier don't ask us to focus on themselves, but help us to grasp the marvel of light itself.

This does not mean that we should efface ourselves and vanish in invisibility, but that we give ourselves as light for others. It does not mean that we should ignore all the beauty around us, in its myriad colours and shapes, but that we let our glance find its way home from all that glorious diversity toward the light where all beauty resides.

There is a little story in one of Rachel Remen's books that speaks of this homing gaze. As I remember the incident, when she was a teenager Rachel was volunteering at a nursing home and was assigned to care for an old lady who would sit in her wheelchair all day, gazing at a patch of sunlight. She seemed to have lost long since the ability to speak. Frustrated at the old lady's unresponsiveness, one day Rachel blurted out, 'What are you looking at, Ma'am?' Turning slowly toward the girl, the old lady replied quietly, 'My child, I am looking at the light.'

Thus we learn this contemplative way of looking into or through or beyond what is visible, of letting our eyes search deep into the wonders of scenes and souls, always seeking that restful poise, that Sabbath repose, where sight becomes insightful, where vision verges on the beatific. For whether the light is refracted through the water of a clear stream, reflected from the leaves of an aspen tree, or resplendent on the face of a laughing child, it is the light of him who comes near to us to lead us home to the One who 'dwells in unapproachable light, whom no man has ever seen or can see' (1 Timothy 6:16).

13

Companions on the Road

I took the bus from Santa Ana, where I had spent a few weeks helping to open a new house of the Brothers, to the old bus station in Los Angeles' Skid Row. The next day I was due to begin my novitiate at Cambria Street. As the bus left the freeway and came down the crowded streets of Skid Row, I had a feeling of home-coming. These broken people – stumbling winos, nodding junkies, prowling hookers, ball-chasing children of immigrant families, wandering homeless people ejected from mental hospitals – they were my people, the grey people, the losers, the dispossessed. My heart went out to them. I was home.

In my early years as a Brother in Los Angeles, I used to work in a day centre for homeless men. Among the various services provided, there was a section at the back with about 30 cots where people could sleep for a few hours during the day. Many of those on the streets rarely got a good night's sleep; others, under the influence of alcohol or drugs, needed somewhere other than hard cement to crash for a time. One of us always had to sit in the back and supervise the sleepers to prevent thefts, to intervene in fights, or to help if someone had an alcoholic seizure.

When it was my turn to watch, I would often reflect on the journeys of each of my sleeping charges. Each man had a story. They had wandered for many years, starting from all parts of the country and even from distant lands, and all their paths had converged at this point, here and now, with my own. Some of them had told me parts of their stories. The misadventures of others were engraved in the scars and wounds on their faces and limbs. Others were complete mysteries to me, a closed book in a foreign language.

I would try to imagine what they were like as children, as youths, their families, their military service or jobs or prison sentences, their travels, their hopes, fears, disappointments, comforts. I had a sense of the mystery that each human being holds in his depths. I realized that somewhere in this world there was probably someone who remembered and had loved each of them since his childhood. And for many there was a friend, a lover, a child who still kept track of them or who wondered where they were now. It was my belief that God had accompanied them every step of their journeys, was watching over them that very moment with me, and was waiting for them patiently at the end of their road, ready to welcome them like the prodigal father, if only they would let him. Lost, we are all lost, wayward wanderers in the confusing tangle of our longings, fears and evasions.

Among those whom I encountered frequently at the centre was Wayne. He was about 40, quiet, polite, apparently on the streets more from an inability to cope with life's complexities than from alcoholism or criminality. He came regularly for a shower and a change of clothes. There were a number of men like Wayne whom I knew by name, though sometimes they would disappear for weeks or months. Later I'd find out that they'd been in jail or a detox or quarantined in a TB hospital.

In the spring I went to visit my family in Virginia. It was my first visit home in six years, and in those years I had become a Catholic, joined the Brothers, finished novitiate and made my first vows. The last time I had been home I was a wandering hippie. This time I was a kind of half-baked Catholic monk, perhaps not much more reputable, but certainly more confident of my identity.

My visit was imbued with a sense of providential inevitability. As I visited the familiar haunts of my youth, there were so many things that, in retrospect, pointed toward the vocation that I had only discovered in the past few years. Even in my home town I had always gravitated to the poorer neighborhoods, and I still felt freer there. One evening I went to the unlocked Episcopal church I had grown up in and prostrated myself on the soap-stone floor that I had thrown myself on in adolescent desperation. The Catholic church, with its Romanesque arches, had the same sweet, candle-wax smell that comforted me when I used to take refuge briefly there on my way home from the dentist or the barber. Walking along the river, I remembered the winter day when I wished I were Catholic because then I would have had a mother in Mary, since my own had died and left me behind. So many of the books I read as a youth, still gathering dust on the bookshelves at home, had kindled my spiritual desire. Even my long walks in the spring-fresh woods reminded me how much nature had always spoken to me of God, as it still did in my new life 3,000 miles away, in the more rugged Western mountains and the drier woodlands of California, with Western tanagers instead of scarlet tanagers, and Bullocks orioles rather than Baltimore orioles piping their liquid notes from the poplars.

After spending some time with my parents and my older sister, I passed the last week of my month with the younger of my two sisters. One day I arranged to drop her at the school for the deaf where she worked, and borrow her car to run down to the camp, some 30 miles south, where I used to go every summer as a kid. It wasn't open yet, but I always visited it, whatever time of year I was home. It had been the place where I had always felt I belonged, even when my father's house had become foreign territory. Not only did I love the stillness of the deep woods and the loveliness of the little open-air stone chapel. There had been friends there who loved me even when I felt unlovable; there had been older kids and adults who took me under their wing when I felt condemned to eternal loneliness. At night, after we had sung the final songs and said the closing prayers and the bugle had blown Taps, we would observe our version of monastic 'Great Silence', although we could hear the counsellors partying discreetly in their quarters. Even then the monastic silence seemed sacred to me, punctuated as it was by the soft, tremulous call of the whippoorwills and the snuffles and snorts of my sleeping companions.

That day was the only day in that month of home leave that I drove a car, and only for those few hours. I was driving down US Route 11 just a few miles from camp when I noticed a hitch-hiker going the other way on the opposite side of the highway. As I got closer, something about him seemed familiar, and looking more closely, I thought it might be Wayne from the day centre in Los Angeles, the other side of the continent.

I drove a couple of minutes debating with myself before turning back. When I pulled over and he came lumbering up to the car, I said, 'Wayne!' He replied, 'Hi, Ben,' as though finding me here, 3,000 miles from our last encounter, was only to be expected. I took him 20 miles north to the first diner we came to and bought us both a big breakfast with my travel money. Then I took him to the other side of town and dropped him off, to continue his journey home to his mother in western Pennsylvania, while I drove back to camp with a smile on my face.

That encounter confirmed the sense I kept having on that visit that my present life as a monk and Brother to the poor was 'of a piece' with all that had gone before. Not only did my new life fulfil the past, but this meeting sealed the connection and cemented the bond. Not only was my Virginia youth brought to fruition in my new way of life in Los Angeles, but a patch from that new life was now firmly stitched onto the fabric of home.

A few years later my journey had taken me to Sicily, where we worked in a small town with a large settlement of Sicilian Gypsies. One rainy day as I was walking home, some of the kids we worked with invited me into the big garage where their caravans were parked, because there was some kind of a family celebration going on. It was an exceptional honour to be invited into the family space, so when I was offered a plastic cup of wine I couldn't refuse. And I was quite grateful to have it a few minutes later when young Pepe, who had invited me in, offered me a piece of fried meat. To this day, I remain ignorant of what it was or even from what animal it came. It was chewy and gristly and a bit fat, and offered as a special treat. I managed to chew it a couple of times and chase it down with the rest of the wine. After I had spent a few minutes talking with the men, Pepe brought me another piece, which I took gratefully and stashed between my cheek and my gums, unable to choke it down, until I was able to slip out and drop it in the bushes. A few years later, when I had moved on to our house in England and was visiting the community in Sicily for a meeting, I met Pepe, now a young adult, with a group of his mates. He introduced me proudly as an old friend, and vouched for my acceptability by assuring them that I had once shared with his family in a feast and eaten with them whatever that thing was.

Some years after that, my 'long and winding road' had taken me, by way of many more shared meals and many more companions encountered and left behind, to a prison cell in Manchester, (England) where I shared something to eat with another man. I knew Kevin's cell-mate well, but had only begun to know Kevin in recent weeks. He had said to me wistfully the week before that the thing he missed most about Christmas, other than his wife and kids, was – 'Guess what! Tangerines! The smell and taste of them. Ohhh!'

So even though it wasn't permitted to bring food in for prisoners, the next time I went in I stopped at a shop on the way and bought three tangerines. If they had asked me at the gate, I would have said they were for my lunch, and in fact I did eat one of them. But that afternoon I went on the wing discreetly carrying a little bag under my notebook, and when I got to Kevin's cell, I said, 'Guess what!' and showed him the bright orange goods.

His eyes lit up and, as he peeled and ate his two, lying on his bunk, he reminisced about his childhood – the embarrassment he felt about his alcoholic mother, his affection for his hard-working father who died of a heart attack at the age of 37, and he paused with surprise, 'the age I am now!'

I saw Kevin again a week later. The trust between us had deepened, the bond was stronger, no doubt because of the tangerines, and I felt sure there would be more confidences, more healing conversations for both of us. The following Sunday, when I went in for Mass, the news in the chaplaincy office was that a prisoner had died in suspicious circumstances, possibly of bad drugs. It was Kevin. Eventually the coroner determined that it was a heart attack, the same as his father. It must have been a genetic condition.

Each of us is on a journey, a journey that will sooner or later take us home. Some of us travel in family groups (like the Gypsies and Travellers we have worked with for many years), some travel with friends or partners, and some are 'lone wayfaring strangers'. Though all of us have companions on portions of the journey, whether for long stretches or only brief intervals, the journey is basically a solitary one.

The word 'companion' means one with whom you share bread. Even on the lonely journey, we have, whether we know it or not, one companion, one who shares his bread with us, one who is in fact the food for the journey, the viaticum who will see us through to the end. For Jesus is not only my companion and my bread, he is also both 'the Way' and the destination – the beginning, the middle and the end of the journey.

The one negative aspect of looking at life as *iter*, journey, itinerary, is that that image may tempt me to think more of where I am headed than where I stand at the present moment. Sometimes I have felt that the greatest obstacle to my serenity is my tendency to lose myself in thinking. And if I am thinking, chances are I'm either reminiscing about some past Eden or exile, or projecting toward some future prison or Paradise. I am either trying to reconstruct some former sense of poise or imagining the repose that will come when I finish all my projects, fulfil all my plans and finally have time to just be.

But the whole point of cultivating a contemplative approach to life is to learn how to be, here and now, in the presence of the One Who Is. If Jesus is with me as my companion on the journey, if he waits for me at the end of my long road, he is also the road itself. And therefore, he is as fully present at every point on that line, that winding skein of minutes, days and years, as he is at the end. From every moment in time, from every locus in space, Jesus is the access, the portal, connecting the passing now with the eternal now. Through him from every *nunc fluens* I can enter deep into *nunc stans* (Boethius). This very moment is the time to pause, sit down with the one who is forever my companion, break 'our daily bread' with him and savor the taste of this precious gift that is too rich for words.

14

A Retreat with the Enemy

I have made many retreats at the monastery in Valyermo, most of them peaceful and consoling, with enough temptation and self-obsession thrown in to remind me who I am. A few have been times of deep conversion and renewal. But I remember one in particular (it was in 1985) that was a dark and disturbing reminder of the reality of the one St Ignatius calls 'the enemy of our human nature'.

Even before I began the retreat silence, the tone was set. After lunch I was talking with an acquaintance in the parking area. She was from Argentina and was telling me that the military regime had interrogated her nephew, a concert pianist, and in the process had systematically broken his fingers.

A couple of hours later, after I had settled into my room, I went for a walk up the property and was passing what was then a pasture beyond the row of pines. As I made my way up the fence on the far side, I came upon a sheep that had just been savaged by a coyote. The blood was still gushing from its throat, the last of its life clogging the dry grass.

Another day, struggling with my own demons and desires, bored and restless with too much time to think, I picked up a *National Geographic* expecting some pretty scenery. It was an issue with an article on voodoo rites in Haiti. Yielding to curiosity, I read it all.

The day before the retreat was to end, I had planned to go for a long hike. I left before dawn, fought my way over barbed wire and around cholla cactus, up and over the ridge beyond the cemetery, then across the Punchbowl road and up along the Cruthers Creek wash into the higher mountains. Just before the trail turned up and away from the stream, I came across a campsite where someone had left some pages torn from a pornographic magazine. Just what I needed – torture, death, gore, devil worship, *acedia* and now, *luxuria* and lust! What was the message of this retreat? True, Fr Philip was directing me and giving me long tracts to read from St Paul's letters, but there was definitely another influence at work.

It was an overcast day and not too hot, so I started up the trail into the National Forest, wondering how high I'd climb before I'd have to turn back. As the path zigzagged up into the pines, I came upon a stretch where there was a sheer drop to the ravine below. I had a moment of dizziness and then a strong pull to the edge. There was no voice, but there was an impulse, not so much to jump as to yield, to let the inevitability of gravity, of hopelessness, of death, have its victory. I teetered for a moment and then sat abruptly on a flat rock, sweating and woozy. I knew I didn't have the strength to oppose that dark attraction, and I was afraid, very afraid.

I don't know what prompted me, but I started singing a hymn. After a few minutes I began to feel my strength return. It was time to start back to the monastery, to that outpost of civility on the borders of the vast and fascinating desert where we meet and discern the spirits of life and of death. I had had enough wilderness and solitude for one day. As I trudged back down the rocky path, I found myself singing exultantly, with quiet joy, hymn after hymn – 'Now is the Victor's triumph won … Alleluia!'

As I sat in the chapel's dark stillness before Vespers, the warm colours of the two brightly colored windows behind the stone altar calmed my soul – the sun-like, announcer on the left, afire with praise; the moon-like listener on the right, undone by the piercing word of Light.

'And all manner of things shall be well.'

15

Fifth and Spring

Just the day before, I had been sitting on a rocky slope in the shade of a large juniper tree, gazing out over the blooming yuccas and the swaths of desert wildflowers to the distant expanse of salt flats which stretched out to the low rocky hills on the horizon. Now I was in the canyon of downtown Los Angeles walking in the shadows of the old hotels and office buildings along Fifth between Main and Broadway. It was about 3:30 or 4:00 in the afternoon, and homeward-bound office workers were beginning to mix with the stream of shoppers and others moving about the streets. This was the 1980s – there were no lofts for rent. Hardly anybody lived down there other than the residents of Skid Row, including us Brothers who worked at the centre in Winston Street, amidst the missions, cheap hotels, bars and warehouses.

I suppose the serenity of my week at the monastery was still not dissipated by the rush and rawness of the city, because I was able to see something that day that I had never seen before. As I strolled along, I watched the suited businessmen and stylishly dressed women, the shopkeepers and window-shoppers, policemen and parolees, beggars in wheelchairs and kids having a snoop around before going home from school, homeless alcoholics and cast-out mental patients lost in their own worlds. And every one of them seemed to be carrying a burden, to be stumbling under a weight. Even the well-dressed and purposeful seemed to have wandered off a battle-field. There were no heroes or saviours, only the walking wounded, limping and lurching along, their spiritual wounds as visible to me for once as their physical flaws.

Each person I saw was engaged in his own private stations of the cross – battered and bullied by blind forces beyond their control, bludgeoned by fate. None of us knew what we were doing, where we were being driven. Each one was an innocent, a child, and each one was a convicted felon filling out an indeterminate sentence. Each one was another Jesus, and Jesus was another Everyman. And all of us stumbled along, fell and struggled up again, at various stages on the long walk from judgment to the grave.

I had never seen so clearly what by instinct I knew was true – that Jesus had truly joined us in our condition as the condemned, the broken, the dying; had taken on his shoulders the burden of our loneliness, our lostness, the heavy weight of our very selves. And only by taking up that cross of self each day and following him do we dare to hope to find freedom from the hell we carry in our own closed hearts and minds.

My vocation made utter sense at last. Truly Christ is present in the poor and broken. Truly to show them care and concern is to honor him in himself and to honor him in them. And everyone is wounded, desperate, and poor – the rich are simply those who can afford to hide their poverty from others, and if they are really unfortunate, even from themselves. In that moment of grace I saw our whole pitiful human species as though through the eyes of the One whose heart we break with our blindness, cruelty, and fear.

I felt that this way of seeing things was the golden key that would make it possible for me to live my vocation whole-heartedly. This must be how Mother Teresa saw the people she served each day. Seeing them thus was what made it possible for her to serve them so generously. This must be what St Francis saw when he kissed the leper, the very face of the suffering Christ. With this vision I would be able to see and honour Christ present in the rejected and the dispossessed, in fact in everyone. The realization was painful, because I knew I was the same as all the rest, but there was a fire of tenderness and compassion roaring in the furnace of my heart.

The next morning when I woke up, I felt only the usual weariness. My eyes were gummy and my mouth was dry. As I faced the day, no insight came to my aid. The vision was gone. I was bereft. How could I make it through that muggy day? The air was thick. What had I done to lose that clarity? What could I do to get it back?

A few days later when I recounted the whole sequence to my spiritual director, he reminded me that we live by faith not by vision, that God gives us what we need when we need it, whether our daily bread or the tools for this day's work. We can be grateful for what he gives when he gives it. If we could store up all the gifts he bestows on us we would be rich in spirit and would not depend on him. God knows we are creatures of the moment and can only assent to his will an hour, at most a day, at a time. We are day-labourers in his vineyard and receive our orders when the time is right. Mother Teresa's work was heroic because she did it not by sight but by faith. St Francis only realized whom he had kissed after he had done it in obedience the prompting of his heart.

Since that day at Fifth and Spring I have never again so clearly seen that coinciding presence of Christ within humanity. In any case, I probably would not have been able to endure for long the intensity of that awareness of our misery. Sadly, I cannot say that I have always (or even, perhaps, often) acted in a way radically consistent with the truth revealed to me in that moment. But I remember it, and it draws me forward, and sometimes I catch a glimpse of the fact that each one of us, lost in our own *via crucis*, if we decide to do so, can step into our neighbour's path and be a Veronica, a Simon of Cyrene, a good thief, a beloved disciple, or a Mater Dolorosa.

And it is essential to remember that, as God bestows his daily gifts to help us face our daily sorrows, so he gives the daily joys. 'At night there are tears, but joy comes with dawn' (Psalm 30:5). 'Those who are sowing in tears will sing when they reap' (Psalm 126:5). What I saw that day was a part of the picture – a part I needed to see that day, a part that has meant a lot to me. But there will be other visions for other days, and a day when vision is fulfilled.

16

Perseverance – Just for Today

All of us who are members of a religious order, I suppose, react with surprise and disappointment when a brother or sister who has been close to us decides to leave our institute. It is an even greater shock when this is someone who contributed to our formation, or whom we saw as an example or model of the virtues proper to our charism. It seems so easy for these people to abandon their vows, although probably it is more difficult than it seems. Often we are not aware of the long struggle that has led to the point of decision. But it is still troubling that so many good and promising people leave the religious life, even after many years of apparently fulfilling, committed service. Thank God there are occasional jubilee celebrations to remind us that there are some who stay. And then there is the list of deceased members to help us remember that there are also those who have remained true to the end – even if in some cases the end came to meet them early, through accident or illness, and in other cases it was more a matter of inertia than of remaining 'true'.

My favorite story on this theme is from the Desert Fathers. A young brother comes running up to an old monk saying, 'Oh, Father, guess what! Brother John has run away and gone back to the world!' The old man calmly responds, 'My son, do not be surprised that many go. Rather, marvel that some stay!' Our life isn't easy and all of us have difficult periods. As a wise old brother in my community used to say, 'It is already a lot that we are still here!'

I remember when I first came. I didn't know if I could make it one week. As the months passed, I kept being surprised to find myself still around. But I just took it 'one day at a time' and waited to see how long I would last. Finally, after several years of annual renewal of vows, it was time to decide whether I wanted to make perpetual profession. I thought long and hard about the various options that lay before me.

I had always been afraid of commitment; so the thought of dedicating the rest of my life to God (or anything else, for that matter) seemed impossible. I was like an alcoholic confronted with the thought of never having another drink his whole life long. That idea would be enough to drive him to drink! But AA suggests that the alcoholic not think about the future but simply try not to have that drink 'just for today'. That, at least, seems possible. So I kept going one day at a time.

On the thirty-day retreat some months before final vows, I realized that I had a strong desire to give myself to God in this way of life, to make an absolute gift of myself to the Absolute. But I knew that the great joy I felt at that time would not last forever, and that the day would surely come when I would have doubts and temptations. How could I take the plunge now, make such a huge commitment, knowing that everything would change? Well, there were still months or weeks to go before the actual date, so I just continued to live my vocation one day at a time.

About a month before the big day, I was having a day of prayer. I found myself restless and head-achy. When I asked myself if this was a manifestation of my fear of the upcoming commitment, somehow that explanation didn't fit. So, since sometimes the opposite feeling has a similar effect, I asked myself, 'What if these feelings are a symptom not of fear but of happiness?' And I realized that I was repressing an almost light-headed joy that I had finally found something, Someone, that I wanted to give my life to without reserve. I continued to count the days, determined to enjoy the whole build-up to the big event, and on the day set for my perpetual profession, I simply asked God, 'What do you want me to do today?' In my heart I felt a calm assurance – 'Today I want you to give yourself to me totally, forever.'

It is a strange thing. Sometimes we think of perpetual profession as a commitment for a period of time, just a longer period than temporary profession. In the vows formula, in my brotherhood, we say that we take our vows 'for life'. But I have come to understand that the deeper meaning of profession is not to be measured in years, or lifetimes, or in any way at all. In this act of faith and love, I am saying that now, in this moment, I want to give God all that I am, all that I have, all that I love, all that I do, and all that I will become – and I want to do that absolutely, totally, today, forever, in time and beyond time. That is my desire. 'Perpetual' doesn't just mean those 10 or 20 or 50 years that remain to me before I die. It means for all time and beyond all time. I desire to be united with my God uninterruptedly from this moment unto all eternity.

How can I make such a gift of myself? I don't even possess myself, how can I give it? I don't possess my days or hours, much less my future. How can I hand them over to anyone? All I know is that I have this desire – this yearning has been placed in my heart in this present moment. And I may lose that desire a minute from now. I cannot rely on myself or anything in me, I cannot trust myself or my 'word' or my 'solemn promise'. I can only trust God and his mercy and his grace. But my desire to belong to him is so great, at this moment, that I am willing to make a fool of myself, to risk failure and disgrace. I am willing to risk daring God to do for me what I know I can never succeed in doing by myself. And so I do it, I make my perpetual profession.

But I find that I still have to live my vocation a day at a time. My novice director told us that Mother Teresa herself used to say, when she was younger, 'Don't be surprised, sisters, if one fine day Mother runs away with a man.' It was not, I suppose, so much that she was tempted to get married as that she wanted to impress on the sisters, in a humorous way, the fact that they had to depend on their own intimate bond with Jesus and not on her. But even holy people know they can't be sure of themselves. The holier they are, the more firmly they are convinced of it. For me, it is better to recognize all this and to say, 'It will be a miracle if I don't run away', than to pretend that I never have a doubt.

In fact, the doubts and difficulties are part of the program. They keep us honest, remind us what we're made of and how much we need God. They force us to make again and again the decision to follow him, and each time we make it, it grows stronger.

But that isn't the only problem. It is also a fact that we change. I am not the same man I was when I first took vows. Even my body's cells have changed, some of them many times over. God has healed me of many weaknesses, given me a certain amount of wisdom, courage, and conviction that I never had before. With these gifts, I could possibly have a very successful life 'in the world'. I could have a much more productive, happy, balanced life now, after all I have been given over these years, than I could have had if I'd never been a Brother. So why not 'take the money and run'?

Some would say, 'How could you even think such a thing?' Others would say, 'You've given your solemn word, you've promised God. How could you go against that?' I would like to think that I am too principled to do such a thing, but I know myself well enough to know that I could justify it to myself one way or another. 'I didn't know what I was getting into.' 'I've changed over the years.' 'The order has changed.' 'I was too young.' No, shame would not keep me faithful. If I am not here because I love God, why would I stay to defend my 'honor'?

What will work, then, to make me stay faithful? I confess that I don't know if anything will work. I could end up running away tomorrow. But what I believe is this – that I have to trust God and beg God and challenge God to keep giving me the desire to be all his – each day – one day at a time. I have to be willing to be totally insecure, poor in spirit, without confidence in my own will. I have to be willing to trust God to give me whatever I need in order to be faithful, one day at a time. I can beg him not to let me fall away. I can plead with him to keep me so desperately aware of my need of him that I will cling to him as though he were my life-preserver in a storm. I can make my commitment anew, over and over again. As I change and grow, as I find healing and new life, as I experience doubts and questions, I have to give it all, again and again, have to feel again and again my own nothingness and the joy that comes from belonging to him more and more, giving him today what I hadn't even received until yesterday. For, if the fire doesn't burn deeper and deeper into the core of the log, it will go out.

Can we do anything, then, besides pray and hope? 'Give us the courage to do the things we can.' We can be faithful to prayer, nourish ourselves with spiritual reading. We can receive Communion gratefully and renew ourselves through Confession. I find that one of the most important things is having a spiritual director, someone to keep me honest. I know I am capable of fooling myself and justifying my own wishes. I need someone who can help me see my own tricks and those of 'the enemy'. My brothers and the poor also keep calling me back to the right road, if I listen to them, if I am willing to listen to them!

Another of my favorite stories from the Desert Fathers is about a young monk who comes to the old one and says, 'Father, I can't make it. I'm leaving.'

The old man says, 'Wait till morning, get a good night's sleep and you'll be fit for the journey.'

In the morning the young monk comes again. 'Right, Father, I'm leaving now.'

'No,' he says. 'Just wait one day, do your work and say your prayers. You can always leave tomorrow.'

'Are you trying to trick me? You'll say the same again tomorrow.'

'Well,' says the old man, 'that's how I persevered in my vocation, from one day to the next. So it was for 17 years, and then I found peace.'

For me it has been a lot more than 17 years now, and I still don't have the peace of total certainty. Who knows how long I'll last? It doesn't really matter – it is God who is the Faithful One. He gives us both 'the will and the way' (Philippians 2:13). May he continue to give them, and may we continue to be open to them – just for today.

17
Prayer out of Passion

One of the two great issues that has focused and energized my spiritual struggle since childhood is sexuality – or I could say 'sex' or, perhaps, 'sexiness'. To accept myself as a sexual creature, to learn to love the sexual energy within me (that sometimes fairly sparks around me), to delight in the particularity of my body and its ways, to understand and appreciate the subtle and complex desires, urges, and fantasies that bubble in my mind and heart – and yet to recognize that these urges and energies are, in my case at least, obsessive, addictive, fascinating and capable of luring me into fixation and self-destruction: this has been one of the great struggles, riddles, koans, mysteries around which my relationship with God has crystallized, or twined. Sometimes it seems that God has used my struggles in this area almost like a pulley to raise me slowly toward himself.

> A relationship of love, longing, desire; yearning to lose, drown, submerge self in other; hunger for fullness, completeness, consummation; desire to explore, expose and allow to surge all the beauty of maleness, femaleness, humanness, and passionate divinity: how to integrate all that within myself or myself in That, how to let all that miraculous potion, volatile yet vital as it is, be contained, decanted, in the fragile beaker of my being. That has been and still is one of the great questions that brings me to my knees before you.
>
> Without all that, would I have a relationship with my God? Would I know of my desperate need of you? And yet, does not all that risk to corrode or explode my poor fleshly being, vessel, vial?
>
> There are long spells when all seems easy and I wonder if the danger wasn't a dream. And then – the storm returns.
>
> And the years of struggle, stress and failure have taught me

so much – have taught me one thing: that behind all and every manifestation of desire – angel, devil, idol, fetish, form, scenario, organ, act – stands one great truth, or two: one, that I need, infinitely, urgently and desperately; and two that you alone can fulfil my need. If I follow it far enough, back through all its manifestations, my need will lead me to you, to you alone.

Because what I need is infinite love – and You alone can love me as I need. Infinite love, infinite tenderness, infinite release, infinite self-giving, infinite mastery, infinite consolation, infinite fruitfulness, infinite union - in You alone is my soul at rest. I need you, I long for you, I love you! Leave me not to my own devices, oh Lord, my God!

18

Like a Thief in the Night

At that time I slept in a little room in the basement of our house in Manchester (England). I had been feeling lonely, forlorn, and useless, and had just written a heart-felt prayer in my journal, pleading for some consolation. I put my head down, pulled the pillow over my ears, and closed my eyes. As I was drifting off, I heard a crash and thought some Brother must be washing his clothes late. But somehow that didn't seem likely. I got up, looked down the hall and saw that there was broken glass on the floor and the motion-trip-light was on outside. Somebody had broken one of the small panes at the top of the door, leaving just space enough to reach an arm in and draw the bolt. The trip-light switched off.

I crept down and looked out the laundry room window and saw nothing. Then he was sneaking toward the door, close to the house, to avoid tripping the motion light. Through the window our eyes caught in the darkness, and I instinctively yelled, slowly and very loudly, 'Get. Out. Of. Here!' A look of panic shot across his face and he was gone, over the wall and away into the night. My shout had been loud enough to rouse the Brothers, who had all come running. We nailed a board over the window, and I thought that was the end of the story.

Except that the next day I reread the prayer I had written in my diary the night before, 24 January, 2000. In words borrowed, or stolen, from poets and mystics, I had written,

> I want to be consumed by my call to contemplate the one, the holy one, the door into mystery, the raptor prince, Jesus, my hero, saviour, heart-thief, Lord, whom I adore, before whom I bow down and wait for fire-fall, tender-touch, breast-burst, surcease. Give me the grace, the strength to wait for you tonight. To wait! Come Jesus, I wait for your presence.

Then it must have been him, Jesus, as Mother Teresa would have said 'in the distressing disguise of the poor.' In this case he was disguised as a desperate addict stealing something to get money for his next fix. What if, as he approached the door that second time, I had said something else in the darkness? Something like, 'Man, there is another way. You don't have to live like this.' He would probably have run anyway. Or perhaps he would have responded in anger. Or perhaps some unexpected shift or shock or melting would have hit him and his life would have changed, suddenly or slowly. I'll never know. I wasn't ready. I didn't welcome him when he came, and that opportunity was lost. But there were a couple of other occasions when we did a bit better.

There had been a creepy looking young man hanging around our house. He broke into the church and the neighbour's house, and was casing out our garage in broad daylight when a Brother took a photo of him with a borrowed camera we happened to have on hand. He made several other attempts on the house about that time, and I was really angry and wanting to do him some harm. But then he vanished.

A couple of months later I was doing my chaplaincy rounds in the prison and Mike said, 'Brother Ben, you must know Rick, he's from your area.' The lad looked familiar, and then I recognized him, healthier after a few weeks in jail, and said, 'Yes, as a matter of fact I do know Rick. He burgled the church next to our house.' Rick denied it vigorously, but I supplied the details, and on another day I brought the photo. He was embarrassed but couldn't help laughing when I teased him about good Catholics burgling churches. I also confessed to him that I'd harboured murderous thoughts toward him. But we became friends, and he met some of the other Brothers as well.

One Easter Sunday when he was out of jail he came by for a visit and a cup of tea. He did a few more shortish sentences, always drug-related, and would occasionally shout out to me as he walked on the exercise yard with his mates, 'Tell them, Brother Ben! Didn't I rob your house?' And I dutifully vouched for his slightly improved version of the facts. I phoned him recently, when I returned to Manchester after some years away. He is doing well, free from drugs and alcohol, married, with a job and a peaceful life.

And then there was Manny, our other burglar. He climbed up the drain pipe in the middle of the night, hoisted himself in through the upper part of the kitchen window, took a few things from the house while we slept, and made off with a fair amount of cash that was out ready for the next day's excursion for the children from the summer play scheme. He left finger-prints, and not only at our house. The police eventually told us whose prints they were.

Again, it took a couple of months before an old friend approached me in prison. 'Did you get burgled back in the summer?'

'Yes.'

'Do you know who did it?'

'Yes.'

'He's my cell-mate.'

'Well, tell him I'll be up to have a chat with him one of these days.'

'He was telling me the jobs he's in jail for and when he described that house, I said, "That's Brother Ben's house", and he said "No way! I guess I'm in for it now!"'

In parts of Britain when you are referring to a close relative, say, your brother John, to distinguish him from other Johns you say 'our John.' So when I took one of the Brothers to prison with me one day, I introduced Manny to him saying 'This is Manny, he's our burglar.' After shaking hands, Manny turned to me and said, embarrassed, 'I wish you wouldn't say that.'

Manny was in prison for about a year. A number of his friends offered to 'do him in' (beat him up) for me, but I declined the offer. He was always sheepish when I approached him. Apparently his mother had given him a good dressing down when she heard whom he'd robbed and what the money was meant for. When he got out, I ran into him a couple of times in the neighbourhood, and he looked embarrassed and uncertain, even when I said, 'Come round for a coffee. You know where we live!' He had been released early on condition that he participate in a drugs program.

Then one day he shouted to me as I was walking home from town, caught up with me, and accompanied me for a few blocks. He was doing well and told me about the program and the projects he was involved in. Five years later I heard from mutual friends that he had died, and I assumed that it was from drugs. But many years later, after I had returned to Los Angeles for seven years and then come back to Manchester, I was talking to a woman newly out of a rehab. We were talking about mutual acquaintances, and I mentioned the story of Manny and said, 'Sad that he died, like that, of an overdose.'

'No,' she said. 'He didn't die of an overdose. He died of a heart attack, young, but clean, and with his family, on holiday. No, once he got recovery, he didn't look back. He died clean.'

I do believe that there is a presence of Jesus, a seed of Christ-life, lodged in every soul. It has taken a long enough for mine to break open and begin to sprout. I can wait in faith for it to spring to life in others. An article in *National Geographic*, after the great Yellowstone forest fires of 1988, mentioned that the foresters had always been puzzled that the pine-cones of the lodge-pole pines always had a few super-hard seeds along with the normal ones. The extremely hot fires of that summer burned deep into the soil, incinerating roots and seeds alike, and every living creature. The foresters thought there would be erosion and floods, and that it would take years for the land to recover. But the next spring the slopes were covered with pine seedlings. The intense heat of that conflagration had cracked open the iron-hard seeds when all the other seeds had burned to ash. They required that degree of heat to germinate. Some of my friends may need those purgatorial fires to unleash the Christ-life hidden in their hearts. I can stand by them in hope and wait for that day.

St Paul says 'the Day of the Lord is going to come like a thief in the night' (1 Thesssalonians 5:2). I wasn't ready when he came as a thief on that January night in 2000 – or perhaps I was too ready. I was like the householder who, if he had known what time the burglar would come, 'would have stayed awake and would not have allowed anyone to break through the wall of his house. Therefore, you too must stand ready because the Son of Man is coming at an hour you do not expect' (Matthew 23:43-44).

Will I be ready the next time Jesus comes to me like a thief in the night? Whether I'm ready or not, he will come. I hope I will be waiting to welcome him, even if he comes disguised. And when he comes for the last time, I pray that he will come as the stronger man he spoke of in Luke (11:21-22), who despoils the strong man, the devil, of his weapons and liberates us from the grip of fear and death. All that matters is that he comes, like a thief or like a conqueror. He can carry off everything I have, as long as he takes my heart as well.

19

The Burden of Self

Most of the prisoners were on visits or at work, but as I walked along the fourth floor landing on chaplaincy rounds, James emerged from his cell and said, 'Hiya, Brother Ben, how's things?' James was a tall young man, a good four inches taller than me, with a shaved head and big biceps. When he was not in prison he struggled with addiction and with the consequences of not taking the medicines prescribed for his mental health problems.

I'm not very good at pretending, so I answered, 'To tell the truth, James, things aren't that great at the moment.'

'Why? You should be happy, monn!' he said, playing on his Jamaican roots. 'You can go home in a couple of hours. You can go to the pub. You can see women. You're free! Why aren't you happy?'

With a trace of exasperation I found myself over-ruling my inner censor and responding, 'James, you have no idea what a burden it is to be me!'

He blinked, surprised. Then slowly he reached his hand out and rested it on my shoulder, then gripped it and looked me steady in the eye with such tenderness and affection that I understood that, in fact, he knew exactly what I meant. We held our eyes locked for about three seconds, then he let go of my shoulder, we grinned a bit sheepishly at the intimacy of the moment and went our separate ways. Of such little shared passions tiny Easters are made, the miniature seismic shifts that reduce the need of earthquakes as our personal tectonic plates slowly move, reconfiguring inner continents. I had felt that sense of burden many times before, but had never expressed it out loud. The truth of it continued to ring in my memory.

I have thought often, since that day, of the recognition we shared in that moment, James and I – the burden of self. Is that the daily cross our Lord tells us we must carry (Luke 9:23)? Analysing the thought doesn't help – if my self is my cross, who is crucified on it and who drives the nails? No, let's not get into a discussion of Freudian, Jungian, transactional or other modes of compartmentalizing the psyche. That isn't the point. The point is that I sometimes experience myself as a lump, a blob, an awkward, shifting bulk of muscles, nerves, thoughts, cravings, terrors, memories, aspirations, needs, and sensations, all kneaded together into one big ball of pitch like Br'er Rabbit's tar-baby. And it is a burden, no question. And I don't know what to do with it or about it.

I know that this bundle of tangled energies and inertias is not simply my physical body; I am not so polarized as to fall for the old Manichaean body-spirit split. Maybe the sense of burden is what St Paul calls the flesh, that is, the whole struggling self: the body and mind with all their urges, pains and spasms, euphorias and ecstasies, weaknesses, handicaps, defects and dreams. Whatever it is, this onus of self, I can feel the heaviness of it, the viscosity, the amorphousness. And I don't seem to be able to get rid of it.

Jesus said that, if we want to follow him, we have to take up our cross daily and carry it, following him; so the obvious thing to do is to carry it. I've heard lots of meditations and homilies on the theme. Some preachers say we don't need to manufacture our own crosses, life supplies enough. Others say we only have to carry the crosses that God wills for us and not those we ourselves or others impose on us. But how do we know which ones those are? The fact is, I'm stuck with this self – I'm stuck to this self – so I may as well accept the fact that it's there and that it's burdensome and get on with it.

Acceptance
Acceptance helps by reducing the friction, the drag – my inner resistance, my rebelliousness, my resentment at being lumbered with this specific load of self. Acceptance of what, though? Acceptance, at least of the fact that I have a burden, this particular burden, and that it is my lot to carry it the best I can. I can accept the fact that I belong to a species that tends to get tangled, snarled, and mired in messes, that tends to produce confusion and to need a lot of help resolving its problems.

Two people in very different situations once, independently, shared the same insight with me. One was a prison officer who had to retire early because he had a terminal, degenerative illness. The other was a fraught mother of five, whose youngest was seriously disabled. Both confessed that in anger and frustration they had initially cried out, 'Why me?' But as time passed and acceptance settled in, they both changed that response to, 'Why not me?' In effect, they saw that many people had difficulties as great as theirs or greater and still managed to soldier on more or less graciously. In fact, I would say both of these people discovered that they were quite adept at carrying their particular cross and that doing so helped them to grow spiritually.

Perhaps for some people the sequence matures one step further, from 'why me?' to 'why not me?' to 'what me?' They discover that their struggle with the burden of self clarifies things for them. They see that much of what they thought was of the essence of their personal identity is in fact superficial, accidental or expendable, and that their deep self is something finer, stronger, simpler, and more subtle – a mystery held in pledge by the *Mysterium tremendum,* to be revealed in the fullness of time.

Thus acceptance eases the process of carrying my burden of self by diminishing what impedes smooth forward movement. Radical acceptance can sometimes seem as revolutionary as putting wheels on luggage or sled-runners on an arctic cargo.

Lightening the load – drying

I may not be able to get rid of the burden of self, but I can lighten it. When I imagine my self as a burden, the flotsam and litter of my being seem to be held together by a sort of thick, clayey mud. Other times, the load seems like a mass of sodden, tangled rags. So, one way to lighten the load is to dry it out. That means exposing it to air and sunlight. People in recovery from addictions learn that 'we are only as sick as our secrets'. It helps immeasurably to find someone whom we trust, with whom we can talk through our shameful secrets and our private terrors. We usually discover that our best-guarded treasures of guilt and weakness are not as shocking or as original as we imagined. Another result of this process is that we learn to take ourselves less seriously – even, with God's grace, to laugh at ourselves. The reluctant chuckle, the hesitant sigh are palpable signs of healing.

The muck that binds our mud-ball of detritus is kept moist by our tears of self-pity, our spiteful spittle, and our lustful drooling. As we expose all that phlegm and saliva to the light of day, bit by bit the clay dries, cracks, and falls away, sometimes taking with it chunks of the debris embedded in it.

Lightening the load – dropping and chopping

One of the first times I visited St Andrew's Priory (now Abbey) in Valyermo, I was just beginning to discover the joys and consolations of a relationship with God. With the fervour of a novice I wanted to engage my whole being in that prayerful self-offering. My mind was popping with brilliant insights, my psyche was soaring with lofty inspirations, but my poor old body was feeling lonely and left out. Consequently, it was either sulking miserably out behind the kitchen, or plotting mayhem and rebellion in some dark corner. When I tried to please or appease my senses in the usual way, by indulging their desires, they took over and hijacked the whole operation. By trial and error I discovered that the best way for the body to participate in the spiritual life is not by letting it feel full but by letting it feel a certain salutary emptiness, unchaining it from its slavery to comfort and satiety. Lying in bed munching sweets isn't the most effective spiritual practice.

Part of the program our Lord outlined for us to follow him was denying ourselves. In our soft age that can sound very primitive and masochistic. We tend to want to bargain with ourselves, or with God. We say, 'Well, I'll give up tobacco, but you'll have to make up for it by giving me dark chocolate.' Or, 'If I can't comfort myself with whiskey, let me at least have wine.' Sometimes I have to recognize that it is good just to say no to myself. That's what denying myself means – simply saying no to that insatiable, needy, demanding part of myself that always wants more.

For many years I went running three or four times a week. First, let me make it clear that I didn't do it because it was good for me. I did it because a friend made it look enjoyable and said it helped him feel more centered. That same friend advised me never to turn running into an obligation but to do it for the pleasure and only for as long as I enjoyed it. He knew that if it became a regime I would rebel. And for more than 30 years I continued to enjoy that exercise. Now that my knees no longer allow it, I sometimes have dreams that I am able to run again, and it is such a feeling of freedom, almost as good as my youthful dreams of flying. When I ran I wore shorts and a tee-shirt, or as little as colder weather would permit. When I swam I wore even less. We strip off all that impedes the flow of air or water around us. What the spiritual masters of old called asceticism is not primarily a way of subduing or punishing the body, but a way of lightening the load. It is a liberating discipline that allows us to chop off the snags and snarls that hook us, lets us drop the ballast that weighs us down, spiritually as well as physically. We can say no to heavy food and lying around on couches, but we can also say no to grumpiness and criticism of self and others.

To deny oneself can sometimes mean more than saying no to oneself. It can also mean disputing the self's illusion of being the centre of the universe. The earthy humour of humility allows us to see the absurdity of our own self-importance. Paul says (Galatians 6:3) 'If anyone thinks he is something, when he is nothing, he deceives himself.' This is not nihilistic self-loathing but the fresh, liberating air of truth. We are little creatures and we are sinners. We are not expected to control anything other than ourselves, and that imperfectly. We are not obliged to understand everything that's going on around us, and there is no commandment that we must be right at all costs. We are weak, fragile, fallible, easily hurt, subject to sickness and injury, often tempted, sorely tested, and neither water-, germ- nor bullet-proof. And, despite all that, we can still conjure up delusions of grandeur! We are truly a marvel in our own eyes! The fact is, as spiritual giants go, I am definitely in the midget league, and in a contest of sinners I wouldn't win any prizes for style or competence.

Sharing the load
Just before Paul said what I quoted above about thinking ourselves

something, he said something else: 'Bear one another's burdens, and so fulfil the law of Christ' (Galatians 6:2). And Christ himself said: 'Come to me, all who labour and are heavily burdened and I will give you rest. Take my yoke upon you, and learn from me; for I am gentle and humble of heart, and you will find rest for your souls. For my yoke is easy and my burden light.' (Matthew 11:28-30).

A yoke is an instrument that allows a single load to be hauled by two oxen. So how is it that by taking up his burden as well as my own things will be easier and lighter? Strange math, that. Mind-boggling physics. But the fact is, when James and I linked eyes that day on the fourth floor landing, we both felt free and we both continued our day lighter and more grateful. Was James my Simon of Cyrene that day, helping me carry my cross, my burden of self? And did I, somehow, revealing my own human weakness, help James carry his cross that day? Were we yoked together? Was Jesus himself the yoke?

It is a truism that sharing sorrows halves them and sharing joys doubles them. So it is not surprising that when we find a companion who is willing to help us carry our woes, our own burden becomes lighter. That is only reasonable. But the odd thing is when the position changes and it is I who help my friend carry his burden, her load, then the true magic occurs. Because in doing so I experience a glorious lightness of spirit. At least for that moment I forget my own load because I am concentrating on my friend's. And I don't even experience my full share of my friend's burden because it is not invested with that whole onerous ponderousness of being *my* burden of self.

For is it not precisely the 'my-ness' of my burden that magnifies the weight of it? Maybe that is the hidden wisdom of Peter's advice: 'Cast all your worries on [the Lord], for he cares about you.' (1 Peter 5:7) By divesting ourselves of our anxieties, by signing ownership over to him, we shed the onus of possession. Our proprietorship of our burden of self adds to it the weight of shame, guilt, and responsibility. 'Left luggage' and unclaimed mail are not actually a burden for anyone. They just occupy space, and the Lord has plenty of that.

Release
The way of the cross, the valley of the burden, is our way home. As I have said too many times in this reflection, life often seems like a burden. It is only fair to say as well, however, that there are days when it is not a burden at all. There are times when I feel free and unencumbered, like a mountaineer on a long trek when he has taken off his backpack for the night. There are even rarer days when I have felt like a kite dancing in the air, flown by the one who made the wind. Those are the foretastes of what it means to be released from the burden of self. Jesus had his Transfiguration on the mountain, when the three disciples got a glimpse of the glory that would be his when his long haul was ended. Perhaps those moments of exultation are our own little flashes of the transformation, tastes of the metamorphosis to come.

When I was a boy in elementary school, Miss Olive Clark used to come in once a week for a Bible class with the Protestant children (of whom I was one). She gave us an image of the new life in Christ which I still remember. Two little dragon-fly larvae that lived in the muck at the bottom of the pond were talking, and they observed that some of their peers would crawl up the stem of a reed and disappear above the water-line. One of them said, 'I hope I never do that. I don't like the idea of disappearing like that.'

The other one said, 'But maybe there's something up there, beyond that flat roof. Myself, I sometimes feel an urge to climb one of those reeds myself.'

'Well,' said the other, 'if you ever do, promise me that you'll come back and tell me if there's anything up there.'

'I swear I will,' he responded. And so one day in fact he did crawl up the stem, settled quietly on his reed and felt the sunlight warming his grubby little form. In time he emerged from the dried-up crust of his former self, unable to believe the transformation. The wet, wiggly little slug had become a creature all delicate wings and air and sunlight. But he remembered his promise to his friend. That is why you see the dragonfly fluttering at the surface of the pond, trying to tell his friend the good news that all is well.

Yes, it is true that we often experience ourselves as a burden. It is true that I am my own cross, and will continue to be. I can make the burden more bearable, lighter in various ways, as we have seen. But it seems there is no way to avoid the pattern. If we want to follow the Lord we have to take up that cross and die to ourselves each day, trudging along the difficult path that leads to freedom and light-heartedness and joy. Perhaps the very burden that we bear so wearily now is what will be transformed into the sprinting legs and swimming arms and soaring wings that will turn us into creatures for whom gravity will no longer be our task-master but our playmate. For the gravity of earth weighs us down, but the gravity of Christ draws us toward the heights.

20

Outgrowing Self-hatred

Some years ago, when visiting a L'Arche community, I attended a quiet family liturgy in one of the houses, where carers form a loving community with other members who have severe handicaps. Among those attending was a small man, who looked like a large child, with multiple disabilities, who was being held protectively by the man in charge of the house. The contemplative mood of the Mass was periodically broken by a bone-jarring smack as the little man struck himself in the face with his fist, his hand literally capped with a soft mitten to prevent injury. Short of pinning his arms to his side, there was no way to prevent these periodic outbursts of self-hurt.

Later, when I asked whether this was some sort of involuntary spasm and what it meant, the community leader explained it to me this way. Often children with disabilities of one sort or another have an intuitive awareness that they are a disappointment or a burden to their families, especially if their condition means they have to live apart from their families. This can happen even when the parents try their hardest to provide a supportive home. Because the children need their parents so much, they can't afford to be angry at the parents, and so they unconsciously blame themselves for being unworthy of the total acceptance that all of us need. They hate themselves for being as they are and who they are, and this self-hatred comes out in various self-abusive behaviours. The only antidote seems to be years of reassurance in the form of loving, unconditional acceptance and nurture in a safe, supportive environment where they can also discover the joy of giving and loving in return.

Over the years, in observing my own periodic outburst of self-destructive behaviour, and in talking with many other people from all kinds of backgrounds, I have remembered that incident at L'Arche. It was like a parable dramatizing the self-hatred that touches so many apparently normal, well-adjusted people. Recently I was talking with a friend about anger, and I asked him if he had any resentments toward God. Without needing time to think he responded, 'Yes, I can't forgive him for making me me!'

Although it is not my purpose here to search for the causes of such attitudes, when I see the manipulative, shaming approach many adults (and older children) from various cultures display in educating and disciplining younger children, it doesn't surprise me that such attitudes are common. For many parents, teachers, clergy, and professionals, their own deeply ingrained shame and lack of self-acceptance carry across in critical or demeaning words and acts directed toward people in their supervision. Sometimes I see parents who seem to think that their main job is to criticize their children. Just last week a young Irish Traveller woman I have known since her childhood was remembering an occasion when I was abrupt with her as a child. As I tried to explain why I had acted like that, she cut me short. 'But the fact is, you didn't like us when we were little.' Though I don't like to admit it, I have to confess she was right. And the reason was that I had learned to fear and condemn that unpredictable, boisterous, exuberant part of myself.

Some years after the incident with the man at L'Arche, I was on a quiet week's retreat. I had been looking forward to that time to deepen my relationship with God, but, despite the idyllic setting of wooded hills, wide beaches, and rocky crags, my thoughts circled around my own fears, anxieties, loneliness, and inner anguish. After several days of this, I began to see more clearly that I harboured a pervasive sense of self-loathing and that my behaviour was demonstrating in various graphic ways that I had a profound contempt for myself. I realized that there was a vast reservoir of self-hatred trapped inside me, and that it was big enough, toxic enough and virulent enough to destroy me, directly or indirectly. It had been stewing deep inside for decades, but I only saw clearly at that point, in the quiet space of that retreat, how deadly it was.

I think I understood instinctively that there was no act of will I could perform to change my attitude toward myself. I had been squirming and thrashing against the pain of my shame for years to no avail. Perceiving it for the first time as a single thing in all its raw power, I knew it was much stronger than I, and that by myself I wouldn't be able to budge it. Because I finally saw good reason to be terrified of its malignant potency, I prayed to God that he would surgically remove it, excise it, do whatever was necessary to free me from it. I felt totally defeated, and my surrender was complete. Exhausted by this revelation, when night finally came I slept long and hard.

The next morning I woke drained and calm, as after a fever breaks. I had already arranged to make my confession that evening privately to the parish priest, who I knew to be a deeply spiritual man. Instead of listing all my faults and failings, all the things I found unacceptable and deplorable in myself, on that occasion I confessed primarily the fact of my self-refusal, this howling storm of self-loathing that had raged in me for years. I knew I didn't have it in me to forgive myself for being who I was, or even to forgive God for creating me who I was. In an acceptance of my complete powerlessness in the face of all that, I abandoned the entire mess to God's mercy.

The following morning I felt as though a large abscess had burst, as though an ugly malignancy had been cut out from the deepest part of me. It was a liberation. I felt that a burden I had been hauling, unknowingly, for years, had suddenly been chopped away. I do not claim that it was a total liberation, because even then I knew that a residue of infection remained that could sicken me again, but I knew that what remained was not enough to kill, or even cripple me, unless I failed to use the means of the spiritual life to continue treating the wound and neutralizing the infection. I don't know whether the fact that I was not totally liberated was due to some reservation on my part or whether because God knew that I needed the humbling knowledge, like the residual low-grade infection that remains after a vaccination, of what indulging in self-hatred could lead me to.

A couple of months, later as a member of the prison chaplaincy team I went to H wing. As I came through the gates, Daz said to me, 'Your buddy Leo is depressed today. He's in his cell. You'd better go check on him.'

I went over and found the cell door cracked open (it was the time of association, when cells were unlocked and inmates free to move about on the wing), and, throwing the bolt so that I wouldn't accidentally lock myself inside, I stuck my head in the cell. Leo heard me, pushed back his blanket and said, 'Hiya, Ben. Come in.' I sat on his bed and asked him what was up, and he started telling me about various recent events, about trying to learn the guitar, some hassles with staff, and some of the gossip on the wing. At one point, for no particular reason, I felt a surge of affection for this struggling brother, and I said, 'Leo, you're a good man. I really like you.'

Of course I knew that he was also a bit of a villain, and that he would do a lot to keep himself supplied with drugs, but I also saw that he was a good-hearted man and, when not under the sway of his addiction, a decent person. We chatted for another 10 minutes or so, and then I said, 'Well, Leo, you never really told me why you're depressed today.'

He responded, 'Oh, that doesn't matter.'

Prodding, I asked, 'Why not?'

'You said I'm a good man. That changes everything.'

Then he added, 'You did mean it, didn't you?'

'Of course,' I replied, and after a bit more banter I went on my way.

A couple of weeks later it was my rest day. I had been up early to accompany one of the Brothers in my community to the airport. He had left for a two-month home leave. A number of losses in my childhood and youth have left me with 'separation anxiety', and I am always tense and insecure when there are departures or changes among my close contacts. I realized that I was in one of those anxious moods, and that I would probably spend my rest day wallowing in worry and self-obsession. Then, for some reason, I remembered my conversation with Leo. 'If my words made that much of a difference to him, what if I said that to myself?'

So, I said silently in my mind, with some reservations, 'Ben, you're a good man. I like you.' I laughed. Then I said it again, out loud, 'Ben, you are a good man. I like you – in fact, I love you.' I laughed again, louder, a release of tension that turned to delight. Then I lay down for my rest-day snooze and slept like a baby for two hours. I could feel a smile on my face the whole time. When I woke up, I was full of energy and had a beautiful day.

The point? Well, there are probably several points in this little account, but the obvious one for me is that outgrowing self-hatred frees me to accept and love others, which helps me learn to accept and love myself. And that is no small thing for one, like me, who finds it easier to believe the more abstruse doctrines of the Catholic faith than to believe that God really and truly loves me as I am, or, indeed, that I am lovable at all. When I couldn't accept myself for being me, I asked God to do it, and not only did he accept me totally and unconditionally, but he showed me that he can no more stop loving me than the sun can stop shining. True, he loves everybody else the same way, but if I can let him love *me* as he wants to, maybe I can let him love others *through* me as he wants to. What kind of freedom would that be?

21

Vocational Vector

I trace my fear and fascination for violence and anti-social behaviour back to my childhood. I have not been able, however, to track that interest back to its lair, or to find anybody or anything to blame for its influence on my life. After wasting years trying to discover its origin, I now accept it as one of those mysterious, koan-like riddles that has and needs no answer. Perhaps it is just part of my personal or human make-up.

Suffice it to say that I grew up in a rather comfortable middle-class family with only a moderate degree of dysfunction. But with my sensitive nature and experiences of loss, I somehow became a bit repressed and inhibited in some areas. Because of that I had a fear, but also a certain amount of envy, for other children who were more forthright in their aggression, more capable in physical prowess, and more overtly expressive of their sensual and sexual drives.

As my experience of people widened through high school, college, military service, and work, I got to know such people better, and learned to like them more and fear them less. I also learned that those same impulses were in me, part of my humanity, and nothing to be afraid or ashamed of.

I was also, from an early age, interested in 'the big questions' that were dealt with by philosophy, psychology, and religion, and even during the periods when I rejected religion as coercive social control or wishful thinking, I had a sense that there were some sort of spiritual underpinnings to reality, and I believed in and hungered for some kind of unifying principle of being.

With that background, when I finally began, in my late twenties, gravitating back toward a Christian view of things, it is not so surprising that I felt drawn in two directions that seemed like contraries, though they had a common core. My spiritual desire for union with God drew me toward some kind of monastic or religious commitment. And my personal desire to unite or integrate the various energies within me drew me to a life of service to those who represented the estranged or marginal parts of myself.

I would put it like this: when I finally took the brakes off and asked God to find a place and a use for me, he set me to work in the service of those children of his with whom I had a natural bond of empathy and understanding and in whom I could recognize the potential for goodness. In practical terms, that has meant working with troubled kids, homeless people, addicts and alcoholics, and prisoners.

My experience in my own life with its losses, frustrations, limitations, and obstacles has allowed me to recognize and identify with the anger, hurt, bitterness, lust, aggressiveness, acquisitiveness, power-hunger, rebelliousness, anti-social cynicism, and other emotions and drives that are at the root of certain troublesome behaviours. While I clearly recognize the dangers of such a volatile mix of powerful energies in the people I work with, I know they are all there in myself as well. And I have also learned, from experience, that all the positive energies and emotions – generosity, courage, hope, selflessness, tenderness, integrity, candor, mercy, humility, and the like – cohabit their hearts as well as mine.

I am still attracted and fascinated by the dark side, let me be honest. There is an instinctive, survive-at-all-costs part of me, which some call the 'reptilian', which would at times love to be as ruthless, self-serving, callous, and rapacious as the worst of them. But I have given charge of that menagerie of beasts in me over to the care of God, along with the rest of me; and, most days, I have the impression that he knows how to deal with it all.

But I don't think that my attraction to the shadow side negates the positive impact of my work and ministry, because, first, it allows me to accept my struggling brother and sister as no better or worse than myself. And besides, I am inclined to trust that God's grace is with me because my heart always rejoices when the person I am walking with shows any degree of openness to grace, to healing, to growth. The people I know who have made such a journey of healing, or recovery, or conversion, or returning to their right mind, have always moved from the cramped, knotted, self-involved paralysis of the trap toward the open, accepting freedom and exuberance of the dance. To see such changes in a person's life is one of my greatest joys.

My own experience, as well as the dynamic I see operative in other people's journeys, is that, to the extent that we can accept ourselves and surrender to God's grace, all the natural and human energies in us, even those that seem disordered or overwhelming, can be harnessed or channelled in positive and life-giving directions. I hesitate with those two words, 'harnessed' and 'channelled', because they would seem to indicate an element of constraint, when what it more often feels like when I give control of those energies to God, is a liberation and an exuberant delight in realized potential.

When Jesus says, 'Working for God means to believe in the one he has sent' (John 6:29), I know that he is referring to himself. But I choose to interpret it as also meaning to believe in the one, whoever it is, whom God sends me today, the one who is standing before me now. I believe that that person is created in the image and likeness of God, and my job is to believe, despite appearances to the contrary, that there is something good in him or her, and the potential for even greater good. I know from experience that my believing in people sometimes gives them the courage to believe in themselves, and to begin to allow themselves to express the gifts that have lain unknown, undiscovered, and undeveloped in their hearts and minds.

And so, this strange vocation of mine, which sometimes seems to pull me in opposing directions, is, I hope, vectoring me precisely in the direction I have always felt called – toward oneness within myself, with others, and with God.

Let me be quick to add that I also know there is real evil afoot in the world, and in my heart, and there are forces that seem focused on destroying us and subverting our best intentions. I know that I cannot afford to be complacent, and that I have to exercise prudence and discernment in my work, and sometimes to seek the help of others with more expertise and wisdom.

And I know further that I need to pray, in all humility, that you,

Lord, will continue to draw me and those I serve in your name, toward your light and your love, and that you will mercifully strengthen us and save us, Saviour that you are, from everything within us and around us that could thwart your gracious plan to lead us to the freedom of the children of God. Amen.

22

The Side Altar

Here I am, yet again, in the shadow of your presence, Lord. On a plank bench I sit again before the cast concrete altar with its oval womb-hollow, in which a small soul could nestle. The brick floor has not changed these decades. Some seasons, cottonwood fluff gathers in the gaps between the bricks; other seasons, trodden leaf-fragments, or snow grit.

The wrought-metal tabernacle flashes enamel patches, coagulate red and the blue-green of deep waters, amid linear shapes: prehistoric forms, stick-figures, the Fish, and the oft-repeated 'X' cross on which St Andrew, the little man, *andros, vir,* opened his arms and heart to Christ's ultimate claim. Some nights I heard a mouse in the wall behind the panelling.

That is the setting. The moment is silence, each moment the one silence.

And from within that metal chest, tabernacle, tent, Something, Someone that hides in the poverty of bare bread exerts a force more powerful than gravity, more insistent than hunger. That power once drew me, from straying, into the Shepherd's fold; from uncertainty, across the threshold of Peter's precincts; from rootlessness to a compelling urge to give my little to the One who gave me all; from hesitancy to a determination to clinch that belonging with undying vows; from temerity to a desperate plea not to be brought to the test.

Then that strength drew me away from here and led me to other tabernacles in distant continents, and taught me to seek that self-same mystery hidden Emmanuel-like in the broken hearts of strangers (brothers, sisters) encountered in dingy shelters, gypsy caravans, prison cells, drug dives, psych wards, and back alleys.

Written back at the monastery in Valyermo, California after some years in England.

Through all those years, scattered like desert rains, times of solitude reassured me that you still wanted me. Again, for a few moments, I sit in the shadows on this plank bench before this hollowed altar, and I beg you, Lord, to finish what you have started – never stop pulling me until I am hidden in the hollow of your heart, lost to myself in the quiet place from where you draw all to yourself.

23

A Memory Awakened

I had almost finished my weekly chat with Chris and was getting ready to move on to the next cell when I remembered to say, 'Oh, by the way, Chris, I won't be coming in next Tuesday.'

In his usual bright-eyed way he asked, 'Where ya' goin?'

'I'm going to spend a couple of days at a little monastery in the high desert.'

He blinked, gave me a curious look. I continued, knowing he was from up Palmdale way (in California), 'Near Valyermo. Do you know where Valyermo is?'

'Valyermo!', as though he hadn't thought of it in years. 'Yes, I do know where Valyermo is!'

'St Andrew's Abbey. You ever been there?'

A look of wonder spread across his face. 'St Andrew's, yes, I've been there.' A smile, a dreamy look, a fond memory, and he began to tell me the story. When he was about 13 or 14, his severely alcoholic father used to drive up to the monastery with Chris and his younger brother in tow – 'to beg food for us kids, enough gas to get home, and a few dollars for his booze.' The Dad wasn't embarrassed to ask for a handout on a regular basis, but the kids were ashamed. They knew what was going on, and they suspected the monks knew as well. 'But the monks never made us feel bad. They were always kind and welcoming. We always talked to Fr Philip and Fr John – are they still there?'

I said Fr Philip was still very much around and that I would tell him when I went up that his name had come up in LA county jail. Chris shook his head with affectionate memories. 'It was embarrassing, but another part of me just loved being up there. It was always so quiet, so peaceful. We'd drive down that little road at the entrance…'

And I interrupted, 'You remember the sign nailed to the cottonwood tree? 'No hunting except for peace!''

'Yeah, wow, I'd forgotten that. What a place! I'll really be thinking of you next week when you're up there.'

Chris was nearing the end of a substantial prison sentence and had spent some months in a sort of rehab unit and therapeutic community, doing a lot of work on himself, confronting his addiction, participating in intensive group work, journaling and really looking forward to being released into an outside program to solidify his recovery and help him reintegrate himself into society. And then the notification came that some new charges were being filed regarding an incident that happened well before his present sentence started. He was waiting to see what was going to happen, if he was going to have to go through a whole new trial and all that follows. (In fact he did, and I lost track of him in the system, although I still correspond with his neighbour today.)

He was a man of committed faith, one who tried earnestly to practise the Christian way of life even in the hostile environment of incarceration. He had found a fellow believer in the next cell, and they kept each other from getting discouraged. They also shared books and articles (C.S. Lewis, Rick Warren, *Word Among Us*, anything they could get hold of) that helped them grow in their understanding of the faith. Lying on the concrete floor by the toilets, they discussed Bible passages through the vents.

Sometimes they pointed out to me other guys who might want a word with me: the kid in the next cell who is depressed and scared at his first experience of jail; a guy down the row who is angry and aggressive; another who has just found out his mother is ill. Invariably when I talked with these two men I felt challenged in my own attempt to follow Jesus. Not only did they express real gratitude for my visits, they also showed brotherly concern about my work, health, worries and struggles. Jail is not a place where it is easy (or safe) to be honest, but these men have learned the hard way what a precious gift integrity is.

The look of fond remembrance that appeared on Chris's face when I reminded him of St Andrew's was like someone opening a box and finding a precious relic of the past, something that opened a door into a long-forgotten room. When we go into that private room where we pray to our Father in secret, we find that we somehow come into communion with all his other children. The monk's cell is next to the prisoner's cell, and through the wall the two can sense each other's company.

24

Landscapes, Lifescapes

This high desert terrain is so exquisitely austere, so starkly lush. I love the way you can see the soft, mineral tones of the gritty soil, sand, rocky rubble, scree between the spindly creosote bushes and silvery sage, amid the prickly yucca stalks and scrappy clubs of cholla cactus. The scrubby plants stand out against the background of grey and tan earth, formed into rounded hills and steep gullies. There is as much death as life – the jumbled, collapsed branches of Joshua trees; the desiccated, antler-like, dead juniper limbs rising out of the living green hulk; and the smaller clumps of growth – dead, dormant or drought-struck most of the year, with their dried yellowish, rusty and gold flowers and seed pods contrasting with the bare soil.

Fr Werner's desert landscapes perfectly capture this combination of subdued colours and sharp forms, resilient life and undisguised decay, angled light and sheltered shadow. I have always admired his pastel paintings, not only because they so perfectly reflect desert vistas, but also because his style is as spare and restrained as the terrain itself. The paper he used is tinted with the pale greys and tans of the bleached desert land, and against that naked background, his sharp, jagged chalk strokes of startling colour exactly catch the rugged shapes and shadows. But within the drawings there are often swaths of bare, unmarked paper which evoke that sense of emptiness, of silence, of openness so characteristic of the high desert. To gaze for a time into one of his landscapes is like a walk in the desert. You can almost smell the pungent odours of dry dust, moist clay, sagebrush, cottonwood; can almost feel the liberating expansiveness of open air inviting you, like the ravens and hawks, to spread your wings and ride the currents.

I tried to speak with Fr Werner once or twice decades ago, but I

Thoughts after a chat with Fr Werner at St Andrew's Abbey, Valyermo, California

realized he was rather deaf. So I was surprised a few years ago when he started a conversation with me at the table one evening. (It was a feast and there were not many guests.) It seems he got a good hearing aid at last. He asked me who I was and where I worked, and when I told him I was a Missionaries of Charity Brother working with homeless people in Los Angeles, he began to ask more questions. At first, I thought he was just pretending polite interest, but then I realized he really wanted to know – how those people manage, how they keep clean, what they do in bad weather, what causes them to be in such situations, how I relate to them, what I feel about my vocation.

The next evening, since the monks were having a community meal, I was eating alone in the little dining room. Fr Werner came in and joined me for dessert, and we sat and talked again – about his art and about my work and vocation. The next day he showed me some of his other paintings, stored in the office. In response to my questions about how he chose his scenes, he told me that he was always drawn to views that seemed to lead one off into the infinite, into the freedom and wide-open spaces … he did not say, 'of spirit', but I felt sure that that was his drift.

His art is profoundly contemplative and implicitly kerygmatic, in the sense that it echoes the Word of Truth revealed in creation: a Word that challenges me to live in harmony with that same straight, unadorned Truth; a Word that invites me into the mystery of One who *is* utter simplicity and unbounded freedom.

My conversations with Fr Werner helped me see a parallel in my own vocation. The people I work with are marginal, desert people, in touch with that naught, that emptiness that nibbles at the ropes of our being. Sometimes I can look at the life of one of our street men or a homeless woman, or someone I know in jail, and I can see that same strange juxtaposition of form and emptiness, of the inspired and the inert, of colorful character and dull depression. Contemplating the journey of another poor wanderer (and are we not all that, ultimately?) is like gazing into a landscape with the suggestion of a dirt track curving off into distant, silent unknowns.

Many of the great workers of charity, including Mother Teresa, spoke of 'contemplation in action'. Perhaps part of what that means is precisely that, as we do what is called for to be a brother to our fellow traveller, as we share our pilgrim bread on the journey through the wilderness, we also look with wonder at our companion, seeing him as a Word spoken to us from out of mystery and accompanying us deeper into mystery – an image composed, impressionistically, of many definite strokes against an empty background and drawn into a unity not by the framing but by the far horizon, towards which all rises and inclines.

Perhaps that is a worthwhile service to provide my brother or sister living under bridges or closed away in prisons – to let them know that someone hears the hidden message of their life; that another human being can ponder their journey and find grace and goodness there despite all that is broken and half-unstrung; that someone can glimpse a deeper meaning to their existence from the sketchy strokes and empty spaces visible to his eye, and can say, 'Amen', 'You are my neighbour, my friend, my companion.'

To discover God in the desert is to love the desert. To behold the mystery in another person's life is to honour that person as the bearer of his truth. And his truth is similar to mine – that I am 'fearfully and wonderfully made' and 'like the grass of the field that withers' – and that my glory and my delight is to stand in quiet wonder before the One Who Is. As in Fr Werner's art the swaths and patches of blank paper visible between the masterful strokes give context and substance to the scene, so, in our lives, we can, if we look in the lacunae, the emptiness, the gaping holes, the wounds, find the very Ground of Being, that No-Thing which holds the universe together.

25

Letter to Mumma

16 October, 2017

Dear Mumma

It's been more than a year since my sponsor Mick (I think it was Mick) suggested I might want to write a letter to you. I've thought about it a few times but wasn't ready, didn't know how to start.

It has been how many years now, maybe 15 or 20, since that time when I was on retreat in Brecon and invited you down to join me for lunch? And I set a place for you. And afterwards I sat on the floor of the cabin and imagined what it would be like to put my head in your lap and let you stroke my hair, let you comfort me. And then it was time for you to go back and for me to go on.

It's been more than 60 years since you died, that 24 March, 1956. And how many days or weeks was it before that that I had the chance to speak to you or feel close to you?

I don't remember the last time I saw you. I don't remember the last words you spoke to me. All I remember is the closed door, and the hush of the house. But I didn't know you were dying. I thought you were getting well.

When I wrote that article about it all a few years ago,[1] I realized that I wished you had said good-bye, given me your blessing, assured me of your prayers, told me that you loved me – or something, anything! None of that happened. I was bereft, just a little boy, 11 years old. I am still bereft, an old man of 73. True, scar-tissue has grown old and leathery over the wound, but the wound is still visible and at times it still throbs.

They took me to Mrs Quillen's to get me out of the house, and she told me that her mother had died when she was a child. So I saw that you could survive. When everybody was around for the funeral, (cousin)

---

1. See 'A Touch in the Darkness', *supra*, pp. 38-45; and 'Terrible Dailiness', *infra*. pp. 129-139.

Patsy and I were in the den one evening and she looked through those glass doors and said, 'She's here. Your mother's here. It was just a joke.' And I ran to see. And all the months I cried into that little pillow you had made me in one of your good periods. And all those years in which I dreamed that you had come back, that indeed it had been some sort of trick, or mistake.

So what is there to say to you? Over the years I have often looked with envy and a certain amount of incomprehension at people who still have their mothers. What would it be like to be an adult and still have a mother, still have a relationship with your mother? It is almost inconceivable to me. That time when I was about 21 and went home with Pete O. to their house in Asbury Park on the New Jersey shore, and Pete got a splinter in his foot and went and lay on the couch while his mother cradled his foot in her lap and picked the splinter out of his foot. I looked at that scene with such astonished longing. Would you have done that for me, your son? What would it have been like to be your big boy? To be your grown son? To be your equal, two adults relating as such? To have been a prop for you in your old age?

I remember when I took my friends Eddie and Malc to a recovery meeting in Hollywood. That 75-year old man shared that he was telling his sponsor that the main thing worrying him was that his 90-odd year old mother was failing. And his sponsor replied, 'Oh, my goodness. How sad. To think, you'll be a 75-year old orphan!' How I laughed. How that put things in perspective.

And that time I've written about before, when the little Gypsy boy, Paolo, in Sicily, was staying with his grandparents one winter while his mother was travelling around Italy, and how he kept saying, 'My mother is coming next week'; and then being disappointed when she didn't. And then the day arrived when at last he came running, shouting 'She's here! She's come!' And I saw how little he was, and how happy he was, and remembered that he was 11 years old.

Yes, I was angry with you. I know that's not logical, but it felt like you left, abandoned me to fate, like you decided it was not worth the trouble to stay around for me. There were so many feelings, so tangled, and no one to help me deal with them. No one. My sister Shirley tried to be there for me, but she didn't know what to say. Daddy – even less. It was so lonely, so scary, and I felt there was something wrong with me. All those years. Till I was 20 and Fr Stevens saw I needed counselling. And how difficult it was for me even to recognize anger, much less own it or admit that I was angry with you. And then Fr S. died, saving his youngest son from drowning, and that brought it all on yet again. What a cruel God he was, this God you left me for! Relentless. Demanding. The word he uses for himself – jealous. Yes, all that.

And though, after university, the army, my hippie years, and my attempt at settling in San Francisco, I finally surrendered to him in defeat, I was only able to forgive him years later because he gave it all a meaning. He led me to the Ranch, where I got to know those kids who had suffered similar loss and abandonment, similar rejection and self-hatred, and realized that I would never have learned to love them and care about them if I had not suffered because of losing you. And then he led me to the Brothers, where at last I knew I belonged to someone who would not abandon me – ironically, that very One who was behind it all, all that pain and loss. Do I still mistrust him a bit? Probably. Have I been permanently damaged? Probably.

Do I forgive you, Mumma? What is there to forgive? That you were so lost in your own pain and fear that you couldn't think how your death would affect us, affect me? That you were afraid you would break down if you tried? That you were afraid of how Daddy would react? You did ask Lillian to promise to stay until I was grown. I do thank you for that. I think I can forgive you. But why, oh why, didn't you say good-bye?

Maybe that's as far as I can go today. Can I say, as I used to so often as a little boy, 'I love you'? 'Mumma, I love you.' They say that I used to shout it as I walked down the street. Do I? Is the hurt still too great? I don't know. I do know, I can say, still I can say, no question, 'Mumma, I miss you.'

Here and now I guess I can say it. I have to say it. ... Love,
Your son, Ben

26

Terrible Dailiness
Conversion in Slow Motion

'Terrible dailiness.' I came across that phrase years ago in a book on addiction and recovery. I found it an apt description of the fact that many of life's difficulties and diseases, including addictions, can only be treated or otherwise managed with a one-day-at-a-time approach. As much as we would like to find a lasting cure or reach a state of stable well-being and long-term equilibrium, actual circumstances force us to manage on a provisional, day-to-day basis.

Survival

In a recent bout of ill-health this real-life, day-at-a-time approach was the only way I could navigate each day's fresh onslaught of misery. With reduced energy levels and a changing array of symptoms, I had to adapt, painfully and experimentally, to each day's new struggle. Some days, between physical exhaustion and spiritual depletion, I wondered if I'd make it.

In some ways, though, it was refreshing to go back to this basic survival attitude that I have had to resort to in other crisis moments and transition times of my life. Perhaps this is the default approach for our species that takes us back to our primitive anthropological roots, surviving as hunter-gatherers dependent on the seasonal fluctuations of weather, fruit-ripening, and game migration, but also subject to all kinds of unforeseen attacks, harsh conditions, and natural disasters. Whatever and whenever Eden was, there was most assuredly a very long haul between that and the emergence of the foundations of agricultural and then urbanizing attempts, illusory though they may be, at long-term social stability.

In the weeks after my mother's death, when I was 11, I didn't know how I could survive the visceral bruising of loss from one day to the next. In my late teens, I was such a burden to myself that I couldn't imagine living to the age of 20. In my first days as a recruit in the Army, I thought the hostility and indifference of the system would squeeze me to the point of flesh-burst. And in a time of conflicting loyalties, I found myself imagining myself impaled on wooden spikes, or my head thrust under the wheels of a passing freight-train. In retrospect, I don't think these were suicidal thoughts so much as mental images of how I felt within myself. And the only way I could manage to carry on was to console myself that this day would surely end, that the next one might be different, and that one day, maybe soon, would be my last.

In one period of my youth lasting a couple of years, I tried living according to the radical approach Jesus espoused in Matthew 6:25-33, 'Therefore do not worry about tomorrow, for tomorrow will worry about itself.' It wasn't so much that I was religious or idealistic. I was simply lost. I had unexpectedly survived till my mid-twenties, I had no destination and no ambition. I was treading water, so to speak, and had no idea what I was supposed to do next. And so I imitated the example of the hobos and hippies, the mendicant monks of medieval times, the prospectors and cowboys of the Wild West, and took life as a journey one day at a time. I joined that whole battalion of lost souls and searchers that wandered down the centuries, over deserts, plains, and seas, of whom the Buddha and Jesus and their followers were the more enlightened examples.

Because I didn't know what to live for, I took risks casually and carelessly. I would lie down in all kinds of dangerous situations, under bridges, in parks, out in a sandy patch of desert, and before falling to sleep, I would consider the possibility that I might be attacked by bears, a rattlesnake might crawl into my sleeping bag, or a drunken thug might crack me over the head with a bottle – and, even though I wasn't a man of prayer at that time, I had the attitude of powerless but peaceful surrender that I picked up as a child when my mother taught me that little prayer:

Now I lay me down to sleep. I pray the Lord my soul to keep.

If I should die before I wake, I pray the Lord my soul to take.

As painful as life was, I somehow had the faith that it would end in some sort of sweet oblivion, whether tonight or at some future date. This awareness that death is always close by, this *memento mori*, thus gave me a sense of balance, at least a modicum of gratitude that I could probably survive again this time, as I had survived many hundreds of times before, the 'little death' of sleep, or of an oblivion achieved by drink, drugs, or some other exhausting surfeit of hyper-consciousness.

Desperation

In twelve-step fellowships you often hear people speak of the gift of desperation. For me that means not a sense of despair but a sense that there may be one last glimmer of a possibility of an escape before the axe falls, the floor collapses, or the roof caves in. Desperation is the last exit before despair. And if you're in a state of desperation and a door opens or a path is revealed or a hand is held out, you take it. That is the 'rock-bottom' moment, the moment of decision. Sometimes the urgency is such that the decision is made before you're even aware of the option! In my case it started with an unprovoked attack by an unknown assailant that convinced me it was time to get off the streets.

We often hear that the safest way to keep one's sobriety (or freedom for whatever addiction you might suffer from) is to remember where you came from – as vividly as possible, with all the attendant shades of dinginess, whiffs of rot, shivers of withdrawal, and gut-wrenching terror, alongside the fact that you are somehow, amazingly, not in that place now. I sometimes share the following suggestion with people in early recovery. Perhaps it is too heady a tipple for new-comers, and usually my words are met with a look of incomprehension or, at best, confusion. But my recommendation is this, that once in a while, not too often because it is a scary limb to climb out on, you pray that your Higher Power will keep you as desperate as you need to be so that you will keep working your program.

A daily dose of desperation is perhaps just the antidote needed for the chronic reality-awareness deficiency that is at the root of most of our spiritual problems. Mental and spiritual well-being is living in the truth, the truth of how the world really is, how human beings really are, and how God relates to both. The truth is that we are small creatures, mortals, sinners capable of all kinds of accidents, follies, and indiscretions. The truth is also that being little and lost, we need help. And the truth is that there is help available, both from fellow creatures and from the Creator.

Conversion

Now, you may be asking yourself, what does any of this have to do with conversion? I think it has everything to do with conversion. As the monks love to remind themselves and others, one of the vows of St Benedict's rule is *conversatio morum,* and that means on-going conversion. In the chaplaincy office of the prison where I work, as I was getting ready to go out on the wings one day, I made a crack that one hears often among Catholic religious, 'Okay, guys. I'm off. Pray for my conversion!' There was an instant look of surprise and alarm on the faces of the Pentecostal and Muslim chaplains, wondering what game I was playing, until I explained that in our understanding, conversion is on-going and rarely completed this side of the grave. There may (or may not be) the dramatic moment, St Paul's being struck blind or St Anthony Abbot's hearing the Gospel, or St Francis's stripping naked, but that is only the beginning of a process that requires many thousands more steps than the 12 that so succinctly summarize that journey of spiritual discovery.

True, conversion is based on belief, on an experience of the Holy, the Absolute, the Ultimate. And conversion often begins with a radical change in the way one sees the world, the meaning one finds. As Gerard Manley Hopkins has it, conversion can fall suddenly like Paul's or advance slowly like Augustine's:

> Whether at once, as once at a crash Paul,
> Or as Austin, a lingering-out sweet skill,
> Make mercy in all of us ...
>
> (*Wreck of the Deutschland*, Part I)

But even St Paul, as an example of quick conversion, needed his time in Arabia and Damascus before he started preaching, and remained sharply aware of his weaknesses (2 Corinthians 12:10) and reluctant to claim certainty of anything of his own, but only of God's mercy in Christ (Philippians 3:13; Galatians 6:14; 2 Corinthians 1:9).

However, being the complicated creatures we are, we can't change everything about ourselves all at once. We're like a rocky piece of ground in which every winter's freezes bring new rocks to the surface, and every spring's digging has to lever them out, along with assorted roots and clods and other refuse. And some of those rocks are too big to budge that first year. We may have to wait a year or several for them to break into manageable pieces.

> With an anvil-ding
> And with fire in him forge thy will
> Or rather, rather then, stealing as Spring
> Through him, melt him but master him still.
> (*Wreck of the Deutschland,* Part I)

Acceptance

My experience of this process is that the changes of my conversion come in a cyclic succession. Some issue is constantly bugging me, some conflict keeps recurring, or some obsession plagues me until I finally give it my full attention. Usually it is something about myself, humanity or the real world that I need to accept in a more radical way. And often I find myself unwilling or unable to accept that.

I may try to forget it or ignore it, but it keeps pestering and festering until I say, 'Okay, I know you're there. I know you're not going to go away. I don't like the looks of you and I don't really want you in my life. I'm powerless either to get rid of you or to accept you, but I will pray for the grace to accept you any way. God help me, God give me the grace to accept this…, or at least *be willing* to accept it. Or give me the grace to give you permission to do the accepting in me, despite me, and on my behalf!'

The acceptance may not come at once, but it usually does come fairly soon. And then I see that whatever it was that I resisted so strenuously, like an unwanted child, has a right to be there. In fact, he often has a necessary part to play in the unfolding drama of my integration. Sometimes I even manage to love the little bastard, that part of myself or my world that embarrasses or unsettles me so much. And if I can get to the point that I'm able give that kid a little hug and kiss her on the top of her head, she's quite likely to run off and play quietly in the back yard with all my other previously exorcised imps.

And then I have a little breather, a time to regroup and to feel some gratitude for that extra bit of freedom I have acquired by accepting the unacceptable. And then the next issue comes along, the next rock rises to the surface, the next problem-child starts hanging around the kitchen door, looking hungry.

But the question arises, if acceptance in general and self-acceptance in particular, are so important for conversion, is there anything that we really must not accept, anything that really is unacceptable, cannot or must not be accepted? First, it is important to remind ourselves that acceptance doesn't mean capitulation. I have to accept the fact that there is a problem, or let us say, an issue, before I can find ways to address the matter. Acceptance is not necessarily surrender.

Accepting the fact that I have cancer doesn't mean that I accept the cancer itself and wish it success and prosperity in its attempts to destroy my organs. In fact, refusing to accept that I have cancer, or pretending that it's not there, serves only to postpone whatever treatment would be most effective. Once I accept that I have the problem, that I have a physical illness, a psychological conflict, an addiction, a disability, then and only then can I begin to think of the proper way to deal with the situation in a way that I discern, with prayer and counsel, will help me live most fully.

Of course, there may be some cases in which nothing can be done, at least concretely, but even then acceptance does not necessarily mean surrender, unless one decides that is the best way. As Dylan Thomas says, we do not need to 'go gentle into that good night.' We can decide, if we want, to 'rage against the dying of the light.' Jesus had his cry of anguished abandonment from the cross before he could entrust his soul into his Father's hands.

Amputation and ambiguity

But, are there things in us that must simply be amputated, crucified, rejected, excised? Both Jesus and St Paul seem to say as much. In Matthew 5:29,30, Jesus gives us the terrifying warning that if our eye or our hand causes us to sin, we should cut it off. And Paul often speaks, as in Galatians 5:24, of crucifying 'the flesh with its passions and desires', and urges us to 'kill everything in you that belongs only to earthly life' (Colossians 3:5).

But if we have to amputate whatever causes us to sin, then the question remains, what exactly does cause us to sin? It is certainly not my hand, nor even my eye. And even though the mind and the heart are sometimes spoken of as the source of evil desires, they do not cause my sin. What causes me to sin are decisions I make (or fail to make) based on the lies, the false beliefs, the illusions I cling to, my grandiosity, my fears, my habits of thought, my chaotic reactions to emotions. If sin is ultimately based on my choice, my decision, then it is a question of will. And God surely does not want me to kill my will – to surrender it and let it be changed, of course, but not to crucify it. For the will is also the source of my decision to turn from my old ways and embrace the new way offered by the Spirit. My will is the 'organ' by which I am able to love God, neighbour, and self.

As I struggle with all that, as I have struggled with all that over many years, I have reached the conviction that I am not always the one who can judge what needs chopping. Once we have cleared away the obvious serious issues or 'mortal sins' in our inventory, those actions and habits that are clearly destroying us and making life painful for others, we are left with a lot of traits with ambiguous value.

Often when I conclude that I must get rid of some humiliating habit or behaviour, friends tell me that that is one of the gifts and blessings I bring to others. My sponsor or spiritual director or friends may be able to help me see what I need to repudiate entirely, but there is much that even they don't have the objectivity, the wisdom, or the perspective to judge. And even if we all agree that some particular habit or behaviour needs to go, we find ourselves utterly powerless to stop it, drop it, or chop it. There is much that I have to leave to time, to the daily unfolding of my journey, in the presence of the One who is my companion, but also the source of healing, the One who can perform the surgery when and where it is needed, or administer the right medicine.

There were three of us chatting over coffee at a recovery convention. A friend of Rick's had brought him to a meeting a couple of months before, and he had now amassed a week free of crack cocaine. He felt grateful and free and wanting more of this wonderful new life, but was saying why he didn't believe in steps and sponsors. The third man, Frank, was arguing the traditional view. But I said, with mischievous intent, 'Frank, you won't convince him. Rick is a rebel and proud of it.' Rick grinned, pleased. But then I had a flash of insight. 'We addicts think we're such great rebels, always doing our own thing, thinking totally outside society's box. But the fact is, we addicts are slaves. The rebel is that little guy inside us that wants freedom, real freedom. That's the one who's waiting patiently for the opportunity to open the door to recovery and do whatever it takes to get free and stay free.'

And I thought of Rahab at Jericho (Joshua 2:1-3; 6:17-25). Was she a traitor or a hero – or just a survivor? And I thought of my own story and many that I've heard. Addiction is like a tyrant who has usurped control of a walled city. He bends everything to his own purposes. But there is always, in every fortress, firm, institution, or enterprise, a dissatisfied maid-servant, errand-boy, secretary, or janitor who, given the chance, will toss a key over the rempart or leave the postern gate open; let the draw-bridge down or disconnect the security cameras. The rebel is the one who wants freedom. The rebel saves the day. The rebel 'acts against' ingrained habits. The rebel works a program, methodically and stubbornly digging his escape tunnel with the teaspoon of terrible dailiness. Rebelliousness, then, is it a defect or, in this case, a saving grace?

Surprises

It was only the drudgery of the daily grind, under the cold gaze of the slave-driver, Habit, that finally convinced me, or that little rebel in me, that I needed to make some big changes. Or perhaps it is more accurate to say that it was against the background of that tedium and drudgery, that events befell me that made me realize I needed to try something different.

In listening to the stories of hundreds of people, it is clear to me that it is rarely people in the daily circle of the afflicted person who are able to convince him or her to seek help. As Gerald May points out, the ritualized routines of the 'stuck' soul allow for very few surprises. There needs to be some unexpected crisis or warning from an unlikely source that finally opens the chink in the armour that allows the first breath of clean air, or shaft of sunlight, the tiny seed of hope or first tendril of the plant whose growth will eventually breach the foundations and introduce life into the tomb. It is not someone's parents or partner or supervisor who will convince them to seek help. It will be a nurse in an emergency room, a prison officer, a cell-mate, or a stranger on the bus who will say something that will give the desperate little rebel inside the unexpected opportunity to act, to throw a key over the wall or open the gate to hope, recovery, grace.

Similarly, when I have gotten an insight or suggestion that helped me move forward in my process, it was almost never something that emerged from the agitations and cogitations of my own churning mental washer-load of soapy but all-too familiar rags, but some surprising new angle or strategy proposed by a sponsor, confessor, counsellor, or companion on my spiritual journey. It's simple. I need help. As long as I try to stay in control of my life, it will get more and more snarled and snagged.

Dailiness

The on-going process of conversion is painfully slow, and each day has its own difficulties and lessons. Some of the conditions which afflict me may require daily doses, whether that be insulin, warfarin, or twelve-step meetings. There are many blessings in this process, but I suppose the one I appreciate most is freedom. Each step toward a deeper acceptance of myself and my reality brings a greater freedom. I have to learn to let life breathe me, flow through me, breath by breath, day by day. Life, health, recovery, spirit – are all things that I'll never be able to grab and hold on to. They are things that are only in us when they're flowing through us – from God and others, to God and others.

Jesus taught us to pray for our daily bread. I can't eat enough today to last me for the week or breathe enough air to get me through the hour. I can't stock up enough grace today to get me through the month. Each time that I admit that I need help nourishes me for the onward journey. The word 'journey' itself tells us that our progression toward our goal is measured in days – *jours* in French, from Latin *diurnum*. We are journey-men, day-labourers, hired for this day's work, praying only for a knowledge of God's will for us and the power to carry it out – today!

One of the responses to the Responsorial Psalm at Mass is, 'In God's will is my peace.' If I believe that God created me for some purpose, kept me alive for some reason, then I will find deep happiness only by fulfilling my purpose, by doing what I was made to do, being who I was made to be. I say to my friends in prison, a screw-driver will not be happy if it's used as a chisel. A Porsche will not serve to deliver cement. The great adventure of life is the journey of discovery – of discovering, day by day, who I am, what I can do, what I have in me, what I can give, and how I can serve.

There is only today. 'This is the day the Lord has made. Let us rejoice and be glad in it!' Yes, there is a terrible dailiness about this journey of conversion and recovery. But as we learn to live in this day, the terrible turns to terrific, and our hearts open to that 'dearest freshness deep down things.' (G.M. Hopkins, *God's Grandeur*)

Praying in the process

God, I thank you for the wonder of my being.

I want to be all yours, but there are, deep within me, areas not yet surrendered to your sway; closets, drawers, and hidey-holes whose keys I have hidden or lost.

There are energies and resistances, there are fears and hurts, there is rebellion and wilfulness.

Penetrate deeper, deeper within me.

Help me to lovingly accept all that is broken, snarled, and cowering in me – even my violence, prejudices, hatred, and lust.

Help me to surrender it all to you, so you can love it, bless it, and transform it all into whatever you want it to be.

I reject none of it but put it into your care to nurture, heal, remove, or change, so that I can be yours fully and freely.

Amen.

27

The Last Day of the Retreat

The retreat discussed here was at St Beuno's in North Wales (where G. M. Hopkins wrote The Wreck of the Deutschland*). I have often felt the 'anticipated nostalgia' described below, that painful sense of loss before the event, when I have had to leave Valyermo after a few days or a week's retreat. So you can transpose the details of sense from rural Wales to high desert California: the smell of juniper and sage; the croak of ravens playing on the thermals and the lonely whistle of an oriole from a Joshua tree; the baking heat of midday sun and the flutter of poplar leaves in the sunset breeze; the views of the forest-crested mountains to the south and the salt flats glimpsed between hills to the north. May the song ring true wherever it is sung.*

Why this great sadness whenever I come to the end of a retreat, or have to leave any place where I have felt your presence, Lord? I was walking in the hills of North Wales on this cool autumn afternoon, sunlight filtering through clouds over the green hedge-bordered pastures of the Clwyd Valley, with Snowdon's crags snagging distant clouds and Llandudno's Orme recumbent on an argent sea. Contorted trunks of hedgerow ash and thorn fill my foreground, and in the middle distance, clumps of sedge and bracken and gorse; sheep and crows, a hawk waiting in a sycamore. And I want to weep. Why?

Because I love it, and I can't get enough of it, and I can't keep hold of it. It is escaping me. Tomorrow I will leave it. Its moment too will leave it in the lurch. Who knows what will stand in this place next year, in ten years, a hundred? This, this now is so beautiful, so delicious to my senses that I want to eat it, taste it, consume and be consumed by it, make it part of me, make love to it, breathe it, be one with it.

Recovering addicts sometimes say that their drug of choice was *more!* More of whatever they could get hold of. But maybe that's not just addicts, maybe human beings simply always want, always need – more! Maybe it is not greed but simply fact. And all our addictions and vices are merely proxies, substitutes for the only thing which is big enough and deep enough to satisfy our need for more.

Just as we need an unlimited amount of air to breathe in a lifetime, we need an unlimited amount of love, care, beauty, tenderness, giving, goodness, meaning. Maybe we are simply *made* for *more* – more good than we can fit into any lifetime. There is only one who really and ultimately has enough, who *is* enough, to fill our need, our longing. Of course, that fulfilment comes to us through others, and we need others, but we also need to let it flow to us from the relationships we have with ourselves, with nature, and with God. Everyone and everything that exists is not enough without God.

But all this comes to us in daily increments, in moments and insights and encounters and surprises. We can only fill our lungs with one lungfull of air, and even that we can't hold on to. We can only digest this day our *daily* bread. Some days, like today, present us with a banquet that we wish could go on forever. Other days leave us hungering and aware of the relentless urgency of our need. And that, too, is a gift.

This sadness I am feeling now, this nostalgia by anticipation, is perhaps a combination of the two – the awareness of the lavishness of the banquet before me now and the awareness that tomorrow's hunger is waiting in the wings. Can I be grateful for both? Wring blessing from them both? Can this sadness lead me to gratitude, this thirst lead me to a spring, this desperate longing lure me to a fullness of grace that I can only contain by losing myself within it?

A chill blast barrels down the bracken, shakes birch-leaves free. Summer's gold is strewn across the darkening fields. I breathe my warm breath into the cold currents. Let the wind carry it wherever it will. It has given me another bracing breath to startle my lungs alert. In and out. Give and get. To have it all I have to give it all.

Have it all! Take it. It's yours. I'm yours.

So be it. Amen.

St Beuno's, November 2017

28

Bulkington Reprise

What drove that poor, lonely sixteen-year-old kid to brave the vast, stormy literary voyage of *Moby Dick*? Whatever I was seeking in reading Melville's classic found me first, and then seared me like a lightning-stroke when I read Chapter 23. I read and reread that poetic chapter as a manifesto of my youthful soul. Was it as much as a year later that, when challenged in high school to memorize some poem or piece of literature, I chose that 'six-inch chapter', that 'stoneless grave of Bulkington'? At various key points in my life, I have discovered again those galvanizing words and found courage to launch out yet again into whatever unknown expanse confronted me at that time.

In my mid-twenties, in the thrall of my own existential struggles to make sense of life's absurdities, I rediscovered Chapters 36 and 119, with Captain Ahab's defiant diatribe shouted in the teeth of his deity. What is the difference between Bulkington and Ahab and their attitudes toward God or the Absolute? I never felt that *Moby Dick* (unlike *Billy Budd*) had any sort of explicit Christ figure. In fact, when I did some research on the great novel in a university undergraduate course, I was struck by one reviewer's assessment of *Moby Dick* as a sort of proto-existentialist novel.

However, as I have been thinking recently about Chapter 23, and contrasting it in my mind with Chapter 119, I see these two figures, Bulkington and Ahab, as embodying the attitudes of the two thieves crucified alongside Christ in the Gospel of Luke. The two mariners suffer the same fate – drowning at sea. Bulkington accepts his fate humbly but manfully, and his ocean perishing leads to apotheosis; whereas Ahab's death is a brutal and enraged descent to the depths, pinned by his own tackle to the side of his nemesis, the white whale.

Bulkington is briefly introduced in Chapter 3, before the *Pequod* sets sail, at the Spouter Inn and described as a quiet, self-contained man of imposing build and character, but one for whom his ship-mates have both affection and respect. Then he makes his brief but riveting appearance in Chapter 23 and is not heard from again. He has no role in the drama of Ahab and the white whale. But Bulkington stands solid as a standard against which the reader can measure Ahab's character as it is developed in the story of the chase. Bulkington's calm, determined welcoming of his fate, the foreseen possible consequences of his choice of a career on the high seas, stands in stark contrast to Ahab's enraged defiance and obsessive pursuit of self-justification, vindicated honour, and revenge. Ahab resents as a personal indignity the maiming he long-since suffered from the white whale's random violence. Bulkington courageously faces life's circumstantial danger but displays none of that *hubris* so powerfully evident in his captain, that toxic pride which is the necessary element in all tragic drama.

What can we say of Bulkington? He is like a 'storm-tossed ship that miserably drives along the leeward land.' What are the storms that assail him? Were these wounds of his past or matters of temperament? We aren't told. All that we are given to know is that 'the land seemed scorching to his feet.' All of the comforts of ordinary life in the port, the harbour, 'all that's kind to our mortalities', were for him obstacles, perils against which he might founder. He cannot risk staying close to land, because, in stormy weather, being close to land is a ship's 'direst jeopardy.' Rather, that ship must boldly face into the tempest, seeking 'all the lashed sea's landlessness again, … forlornly rushing into peril, … her only friend her bitterest foe.'

Bulkington needed the freedom of the open sea. He was, for whatever reason, by nature or experience, one who glimpsed the fact that 'all deep earnest thinking is but the intrepid effort of the soul to keep the open independence of her sea while the wildest winds of heaven and earth conspire to cast her on the treacherous, slavish shore.'

He was one for whom the spiritual freedom symbolized by the open seas was his greatest need. This was, as Viktor Frankl so famously clarified in *Man's Search for Meaning*, not just a 'freedom from' (from the shackles of self and social convention) but a 'freedom for' – but for what? Freedom to give himself to the transcendent, freedom to dedicate himself to the highest truth – 'for as in landlessness alone resides the highest truth, shoreless, indefinite as God, so better is it to perish in that howling infinite than be ingloriously dashed upon the lee, even if that were safety.'

In this context, the word 'indefinite' does not mean what it has come to mean now, vague or ill-defined, but rather, 'without defining limits', in other words, infinite. Bulkington seems to feel within his bones a need to search out a truth that will stand firm against all the shifting shapes of the watery world which is his field of battle, firm against even the sheltering solidity of rocks, land and harbours. He needs to touch, to engage with, to give himself to the ultimate, to deep truth.

And what of this perishing? Is Bulkington's death necessary? Was it inevitable that he meet his end in this way? Could he have found some inner, mystic seas in which to pursue his freedom, his search for Truth? Would old age have delivered him from his need to be free of the tempting comforts of home and hearth? Is his death unprepared? In his last moments does he suffer terror and cold as the icy, briny swells of the North Atlantic foam over him and claim him and his sodden wrappings? Or is his death instantaneous, painless and fearless, from the spray of which his apotheosis leaps straight up?

Is Bulkington a Christ figure? Or is he an Enoch, one who vanishes into oblivion? Is he like the tall, stern nun in Manley Hopkins' masterwork who shouted out Christ's coming as the *Deutschland* foundered and sank. Or is he like Thomas Merton at the end of *Seven Storey Mountain*, with his vision of the burnt men? And what is his apotheosis? Is he god-like? Is he a hero? Is he assumed, like Elijah, though not in chariots of fire, but by the foaming stallions of the deeps? Is his death an absurdity, a martyrdom, a sacrifice, a shout of victory?

Of course, I can't say. I don't know what was in the mind of Melville, or in that of Ishmael, the raconteur of the story. (I uncomfortably confess, to descend from the sublime to the ridiculous, that Ishmael reminds me a bit of the cockroach, Archy, in the Don Marquis story *Archy and Mehitabel*, who envied the moth's exuberant fascination with the flame that would be his death, though Archy himself 'would rather have half the happiness and twice the longevity.')

I do not need to know anyone else's interpretation, not even the author's. For me as a teen-aged boy, and again and again through the years since that first reading, Chapter 23 has been like a shrine to which I have made occasional pilgrimages, at times when I needed the courage to confront some new unknown. Bulkington's example invites me to face the ultimate mystery, which you can call God or the Transcendent, the Unknowable, the Ineffable. That *mysterium tremendum* can be terrifyingly demanding and yet can prodigally welcome a humble soul (as Hopkins says, 'Hast thy dark descending and most art merciful then.'). The way that Melville uses the word 'apotheosis' implies that this perishing is not a Lear-like madness nor an Ahab-like act of absurd defiance, but that it achieves its end, which is not obliteration or reincarnation, not annihilation or resurgence, but consummation, or, in the language of the contemplative tradition, union with the Mystery.

When I started to write this piece a couple of years ago, I did not know that Chapter 23 was waiting to invite me to visit it yet again. But in recent months, as I have wrestled more and more with the awareness of advancing age, I see that Bulkington still speaks to my heart.

What, he asks, if I approach my remaining years, whatever they may hold, not as a denouement but as an adventure, an exploration of another new terrain, full of perils, yes, but also offering exhilarating new challenges? If I welcome each new day like I did as a child, as a garden full of wonders; if I face my finality with as much sincere (though faltering) passion as I did my adolescent yearnings; if I explore the new territories I face now with the same fateful resolve as when I submitted to conscription in a time of war, and after that, recklessly embarked on my youthful travels; if I learn the lessons seniority has for me with the same adventurous spirit as when I strayed into the frightening waters of commitment and self-gift; if I awaken to the days to come with the same openness as I have done at times throughout my past; can I not take heart again from Bulkington and venture into the unknown with steady confidence that the Mystery always remains? The wild, uncharted vastness of Deep Truth calls me still.

29

Heart to Heart

I've heard prospective parents say how much it moved them to see the scan of their baby's little heartbeat and its tiny squirmings in the womb. But I was surprised to find myself touched by a sort of tender pity when, at the cardiologist's for a routine check, I saw, on the screen, the image of my throbbing heart.

How faithfully, bravely and thanklessly the poor little thing does its humble work, driven by the head-strong demands of an arrogant and self-absorbed task-master, a mind intent only on its own churning thoughts and emotions, its own frenetic chase, ambitions and evasions.

But at my beginning, God set my poor heart to do its job, and so it does, minute by minute, year by year, quietly, uncomplainingly responding to the pressures of its bearer's outer and inner dramas and distractions; carrying the weight of its master's worries, woes and wonders; adjusting obediently to the burdens of its driver's varying freight of effort, responsibility and repose.

When the Eastern Christians speak of praying with the mind in the heart, they are perhaps hoping that the frenzy and fury of the mind will learn some lessons sitting silently at the foot of the heart, example as it is of constancy and patient endurance. And when Cardinal Newman chose as his motto *Cor ad cor loquitur* – heart speaks to heart – he was perhaps hoping that the human mind at prayer, when humble enough to attend the calm but steady drumming of the heart, would learn to murmur its longings softly to the heart of the One who says, 'Come unto me, for I am meek and humble of heart.' And perhaps he was hoping further that the human heart would listen and learn to move in synchrony with the heartbeat of the One whose love is the life-giving pulse and impulse of all that lives.

My mind has much too much to say. Let my poor heart have its turn. I see, on the doctor's screen, my heart humbly carrying on its labours in its dark hold, and I know it needs to speak its wordless psalm of gratitude, of loyalty, of devotion – and perhaps at times of sorrow and of pain – to the One who hears the deepest longings of our souls. And the heart of Jesus longs to listen and to give my heart the comfort and consolation that I so often forget or don't know how to give. Let me hush my loud self-proclamation for a while, and listen to that inner colloquy, as *cor ad cor loquitur* – that intimate converse between my poor, long-suffering heart and the heart of Jesus, fount of peace, spring of joy.

And when my little heart pumps its final round and rests at last, may your gracious Heart, dear Lord, blend my heart's little rhythm into yours, prolong the tympany, swell the pulse of praise, 'as deep calls to deep in the roar of mighty waters'.

Amen.

Postlude
A Song for the Way

If you who are reading this have stayed with me through all these pages, I think I can call you 'Friend'. When I thought about writing a book, I wanted to write something that would have cheered, comforted, and encouraged my younger self, as well as any other searching soul who wandered in confusion like that poor, lost child. We are all in this together, and those who are sure of themselves, and sure they know how to navigate life's challenges, will, I believe, even if it is in their last breath, realize their lostness and their need. And that is, ironically, the precious gift God has in store for all his beloved children. 'Turn to me and live' (see Isaiah 45:22 and 55:3).

So I have written these chapters assuming that those who will be drawn to read them will be searchers, too, and that my process and my discoveries will make some sense to them, and possibly help them, either to carry on, or at least to avoid some of the traps and blind alleys I have stumbled into.

So many of the lessons I have learned and shared with you, Friend, I came to understand in times of rest, times of silence, repose, retreat. Is that not what Sabbath is about? The gift of time to reflect, to ponder, to absorb, to understand? I have always needed, even daily, time to digest, to process the happenings and feelings of the journey.

There is an incident from one of my retreats that I want to share with you, consisting of two little moments, before we come to the end of this time together. It was a retreat I made some years ago in a village in Compiegne, in the north of France. The memory has come to mind because of a conversation I had yesterday, a phone call from an old friend who has been detained for many years in secure psychiatric facilities. It seems that finally there is hope that he will progress to a sort of half-way house, but everything is taking a long time to fall into place. And he wavers between bravely hoping for the best, despite years of set-backs, disappointments, and delays, and a mood of hopelessness and defeat. And he asked me, 'Do you have bad days? Days when it seems everything is against you, and that even God has forgotten you?'

And I said, 'Of course I do. That is part of the human condition. Even Jesus cried "My God, my God, why have you abandoned me?" But moods and feelings are like the weather, they come and go, they're always changing. Chances are, Michael, tomorrow you'll feel your usual chirpy self. Remember the saying, "This too shall pass."'

During the retreat I want to tell you about, I was in one of those dark moods. I was restless and depressed, confused and uncertain what I was supposed to do with life, feeling no energy, no interest, no hope. I was looking at life through a purple filter, and discordant funereal music was playing in the sound-track of my mind. My life seemed meaningless, my work seemed fruitless, every effort was drudgery, and I faced the future with dread. I was burdened with responsibilities I didn't want, and troubled by temptations I had lost the will to resist.

I have discovered over the years that my worst days, my most desperate moods, are when I feel stuck, trapped, paralyzed, unable to move forward. And that is the state I was in at that moment. I had to do something. I was like a cornered rat, like a panicked escapee from a madhouse. All I could think to do was run. Leave it all behind and go! Go where? It didn't matter. Back to the old miseries I had long ago left behind? Even they seemed preferable to this impossible storm of contradictory feelings and insatiable cravings.

It was about 9 o'clock at night. I grabbed a few basics and shoved them in my back pack, and I left, no note, no farewell. I would disappear into the night, down the road, into the oblivion of some grim city. Lose myself in what? In whatever! I headed for the highway, intending to hitch a lift with anybody going anywhere.

But there was almost no traffic. Not 10 minutes down the road it began to drizzle. A few minutes further I came to a petrol station which was open but had no customers. It did, however have a large German shepherd dog prowling the forecourt – unchained. And then it started to rain more heavily. Half crying and half laughing, I turned back, returned to the house and my room, glad that I hadn't locked the door. Defeated. By something so insignificant as a little inclement weather and a dog. What a light-weight! What a pathetic excuse of a man! But despite all that, relieved. I dried my hair and changed my sodden clothes, made a cup of hot tea and crawled into bed. Exhausted.

The next day I was somewhat subdued, but continued grumping and grousing with God all day. It was a rainy day and I was stuck inside. And at one point, the following conversation took place between me and God. I'm not saying I heard a voice or saw a face. You can call it imaginative prayer or something more. But for me it had the ring of authenticity, the taste of truth – the rusty taste of blood or burgundy. The conversation went like this:

Me   What do you *want* from me?
God   Do you really want to know?
Me   Of course.
God   (Quietly) Everything.
Me   (Flat tone) Right.
God   (With a twinkle in his eye) That's not so much.
Me   Cute.

I had to laugh. And now, when I think back on it, I have to admit, you got me that time, Lord. You scored a goal on that one. Tell me you don't have a sense of humour, and a mischievous one at that! Yes, all those times I said I wanted to diminish, become less, be nothing, be nobody, vanish like Lao Tzu into the west, like Enoch when God took him. 'Not so much.' You hit the nail on the head. Who am I? Not much. What is all this drama about? Not much. What did I expect, what *do* I expect. I don't even know. Yes, Lord, you win. Again. And I'm glad. Thanks. I give up. I give in. I give. What? Everything. The lot. And, that's not so much. In fact, it's very little indeed.

Back then, the conversation continued:

Me   I want to be important!
God   You're important to me.
Me   Everybody's important to you.
God   Mmmmm (agreeing). Take it or leave it.

And then, sometime later in the day:

Me   Right, so we've had a nice afternoon – rainy, dreary, a bit of a fight, a few laughs.
God   It's been nice.
Me   But now let's be serious for a minute. Please just tell me what you want from me.
God   Come on, do you really think I'm gonna answer that?
Me   I can't go on with all this uncertainty.
God   You can't? Look, tomorrow I'll tell you what I want tomorrow. The day after I'll tell you what I want then. (Earnestly) Don't you trust me?
Me   No! (Both burst out laughing – brief pause) No, you're too tricky.
God   (Smiling) You're right.
Me   But I do love you.
God   (Very seriously) No. On the contrary. I love *you*!

Coming back to the present, as I said before, my worst days are when I feel stuck. And all I have to do to break the dark spell is – what? Be willing to do something positive, be willing to take the next step, to do something, 'not choose not to be.' Surrender. Surrender to life, to love … to laughter? Yes, and so I return to the right road, willing to move forward in the way Jesus leads me, in the Way Jesus *is* for me, one day at a time, praying to be led in the right direction even if I don't know where. 'Lord, please, just stay with me! Don't let me go! You are my Way, my Truth, My Life. You are my road, my companion, and my destination. Come on. Let's go.'

❧

All I know, and all I need to know, is that there is One Who Is.

All I believe, and all I need to believe, is that the energy of his Being is Love.

All I want, and all I need to want, is to lose myself in That One.

All I trust, and all I need to trust, is that You, Jesus, are the Way to That One.

That is my song, and I want to sing it with all my soul. But I also want to join my voice with that of every other searching soul, and an old hymn says it well:

> I heard the voice of Jesus say,
> 'I am this dark world's light;
> Look unto me, thy morn shall rise,
> And all thy day be bright.'
> I looked to Jesus, and I found
> In him my star, my sun;
> And in that light of life I'll walk
> Till travelling days are done.
>
> Horatius Bonar (1808-1889)

Ackowledgements

The author and the publishers are grateful for the permission to re-publish given by the editors of the magazines where the articles on which this work is based, first appeared. In preparing this collection, the author has made changes and additions to the versions previously published.

To the editor of *Valyermo Chronicle* for 'Silence or a Song' (No. 233, Autumn 2011); 'Man of the Road' (No 228, Spring 2010); 'Musings of a Wannabe Monk' (No. 224, Spring 2009); 'Seeing Light' (No. 243, Autumn 2014); 'A Retreat with the Enemy' (No. 226, Autumn 2009); 'Fifth and Spring' (No. 235, Spring 2012); 'Like a Thief in the Night' (No. 239, Summer 2013); 'The Burden of Self' (No. 241, Lent 2014); 'The Side Altar' (No. 220, Summer 2008); 'A Memory Awakened' (No. 222, Winter 2008); 'Landscapes, Lifescape' (No. 231, Spring 2011); 'Bulkington Reprise' (No. 264, Summer 2020).

To the editor of *Human Development* for 'Journey' (Vol. 40, No. 2, Winter 2020); 'A Touch in the Darkness' (Vol. 32, No. 2, Summer 2011); 'A Dangerous Gift' (Vol. 40, No. 4, Summer 2020); 'Companions on the Road' (Vol. 41, No. 2, Winter 2021); 'Perseverance Just for Today' (Vol. 31, No. 3, Fall 2010); 'Prayer Out of Passion' (Vol. 28, No. 4, December 2007, anonymously); 'Vocational Vector' (Vol. 43, No. 2, 2023); 'Letter to Mumma' (Vol. 38, No. 3, Spring 2018); 'Terrible Dailiness' (Vol. 38, No. 4, Summer 2018).

To the editor of *The Afterglow* for 'Silence' (No. 8, November 1990).

To the editor of *Spirituality* for 'Venturing Outdoors' (Vol. 27, No. 157, July/August 2021); 'The Trouble with Friends' (Vol. 25, No. 145, July/August 2019); 'Seeds from Plastic Flowers" (Vol. 22, No. 128, September/October 2016); 'Being Nothing' (Vol. 27, No. 154, January/February 2021); 'Gazing into Night' (Vol. 20, No. 117, November/December 2014); 'Out-growing Self-hatred' (Vol. 21, No. 18, January/February 2015); 'The Last Day of the Retreat' (Vol. 24, No. 136, January/February 2018; 'Heart to Heart' (Vol. 28, No. 165, November/December 2022).

To the Abbot of St Andrew's Abbey, Valyermo, California, for permission to carry on the front cover a reproduction of a painting by Fr Werner Papeians de Morchoven, O.S.B., of St Andrew's Abbey.